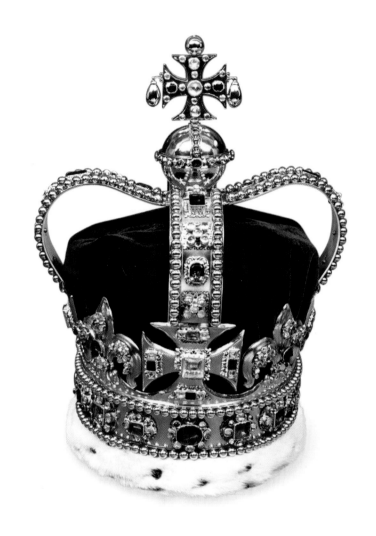

TIME

The Royal Family

Britain's resilient monarchy celebrates
Elizabeth II's 60-year reign

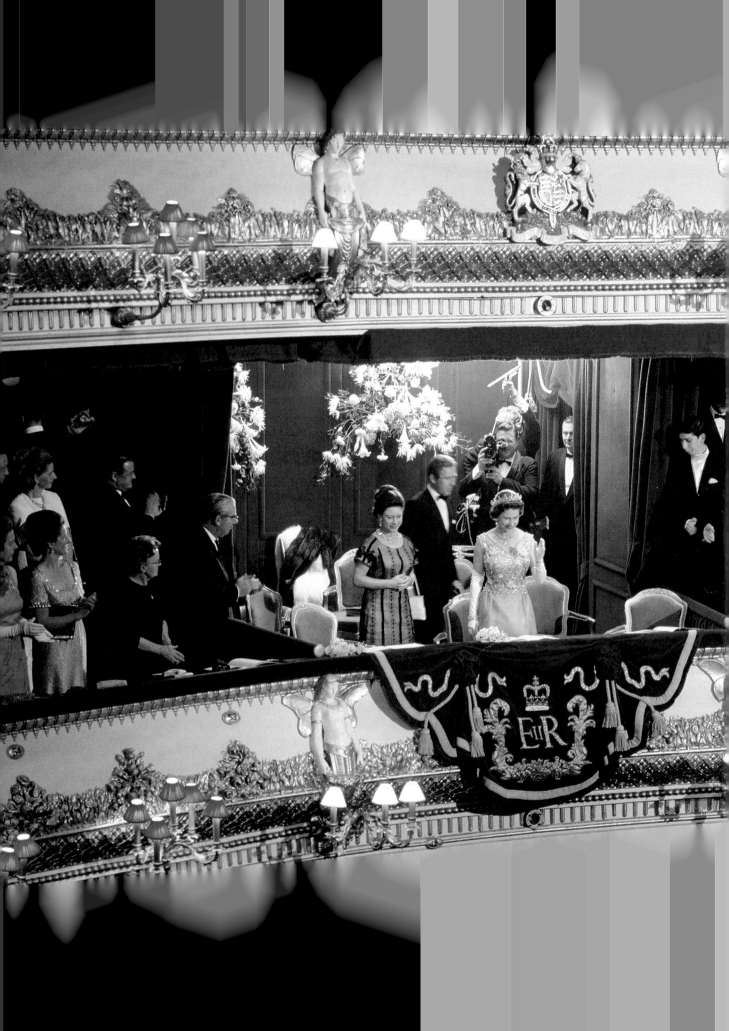

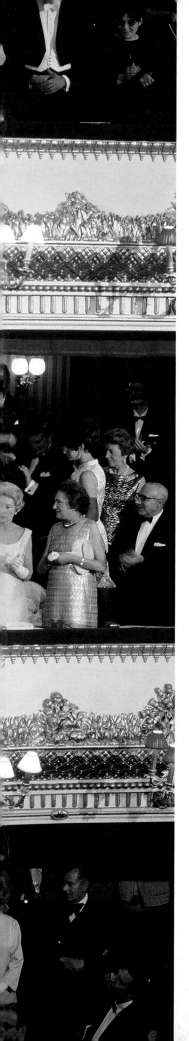

TIME

MANAGING EDITOR Richard Stengel
DESIGN DIRECTOR D.W. Pine
DIRECTOR OF PHOTOGRAPHY Kira Pollack

The Royal Family

Britain's resilient monarchy celebrates Elizabeth II's 60-year reign

EDITOR Charlotte Greensit
DESIGNER Sharon Okamoto
PHOTO EDITOR Dot McMahon
RESEARCHER Elizabeth L. Bland
COPY EDITOR Kathleen A. Kelly
EDITORIAL PRODUCTION Lionel P. Vargas
GRAPHICS EDITOR Lon Tweeten

TIME HOME ENTERTAINMENT
PUBLISHER Richard Fraiman
VICE PRESIDENT, BUSINESS DEVELOPMENT AND STRATEGY Steven Sandonato
EXECUTIVE DIRECTOR, MARKETING SERVICES Carol Pittard
EXECUTIVE DIRECTOR, RETAIL AND SPECIAL SALES Tom Mifsud
EXECUTIVE PUBLISHING DIRECTOR Joy Butts
DIRECTOR, BOOKAZINE DEVELOPMENT AND MARKETING Laura Adam
FINANCE DIRECTOR Glenn Buonocore
ASSISTANT GENERAL COUNSEL Helen Wan
ASSISTANT DIRECTOR, SPECIAL SALES Ilene Schreider
BOOK PRODUCTION MANAGER Suzanne Janso
DESIGN AND PREPRESS MANAGER Anne-Michelle Gallero
BRAND MANAGER Michela Wilde
ASSOCIATE BRAND MANAGER Isata Yansaneh

EDITORIAL DIRECTOR Stephen Koepp

SPECIAL THANKS TO:
Christine Austin, Jeremy Biloon, Jim Childs, Susan Chodakiewicz, Rose Cirrincione, Jacqueline Fitzgerald, Carrie Hertan, Hillary Hirsch, Christine Font, Jenna Goldberg, Lauren Hall Clark, Amy Mangus, Robert Marasco, Kimberly Marshall, Amy Migliaccio, Nina Mistry, Tara Rice, Dave Rozzelle, Adriana Tierno, Alex Voznesenskiy, Vanessa Wu, TIME Imaging

ISBN 13: 978-1-60320-249-7
ISBN 10: 1-60320-249-8
Library of Congress Control Number: 2012931017

We welcome your comments and suggestions about TIME Books. Please write to us at:
TIME Books, Attention: Book Editors, P.O. Box 11016, Des Moines, IA 50336-1016

If you would like to order any of our hardcover Collector's Edition books, please call us at 1-800-327-6388, Monday through Friday, 7 a.m. to 8 p.m., or Saturday, 7 a.m. to 6 p.m., Central Time.

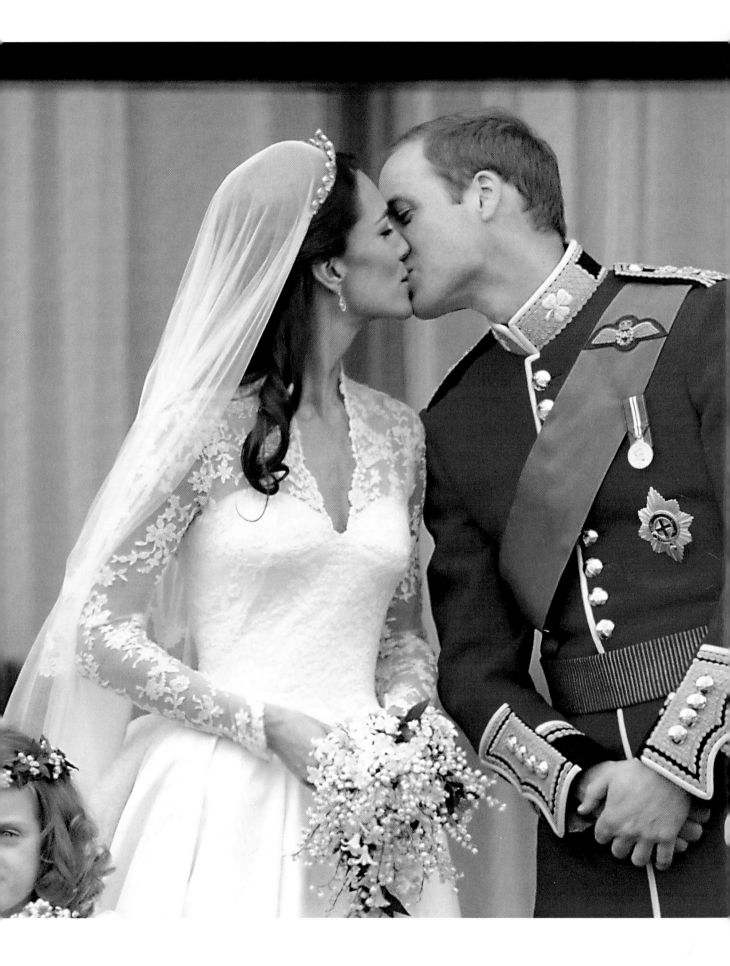

Contents

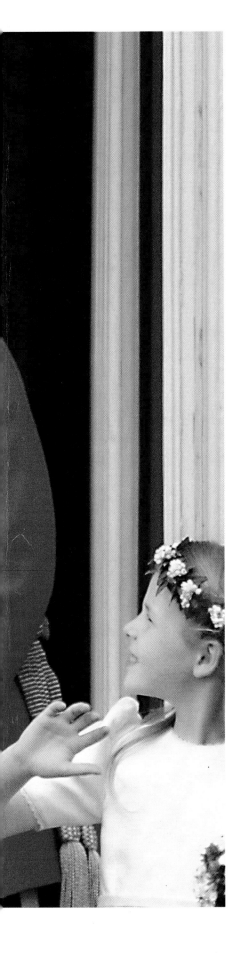

The wedding of Prince William and Catherine Middleton, April 29, 2011, helped burnish the reputation of the royal family

God Save The Queen!

She pledged that her whole life would be devoted to serving her people. She's kept her promise.

By Allison Pearson

She disdains celebrity, but has one of the most famous faces on the planet. She has been in the international limelight for 60 years and has only once shown any strong emotion in public, shedding a tear when they took away her yacht. She has been a remarkable mother figure to her country, but less successful as an actual mother to her own children, three of whom have entered into marriages that could have filled an entire season of *Jerry Springer*. She is unfathomably rich, but she stores her cereal in stay-fresh Tupperware containers and eats breakfast off mismatched crockery. She prefers the company of dogs and horses, perhaps because they have no idea who she is. In repose, her face is a doughy scowl, exactly like her German grandmother's, but when she smiles it is as though a blessing has been bestowed. As figureheads go, she is diminutive, yet she can alter every molecule in a room just by en-

Allison Pearson is an award-winning journalist and author. She is a columnist for The Daily Telegraph *and author of* I Don't Know How She Does It *and* I Think I Love You

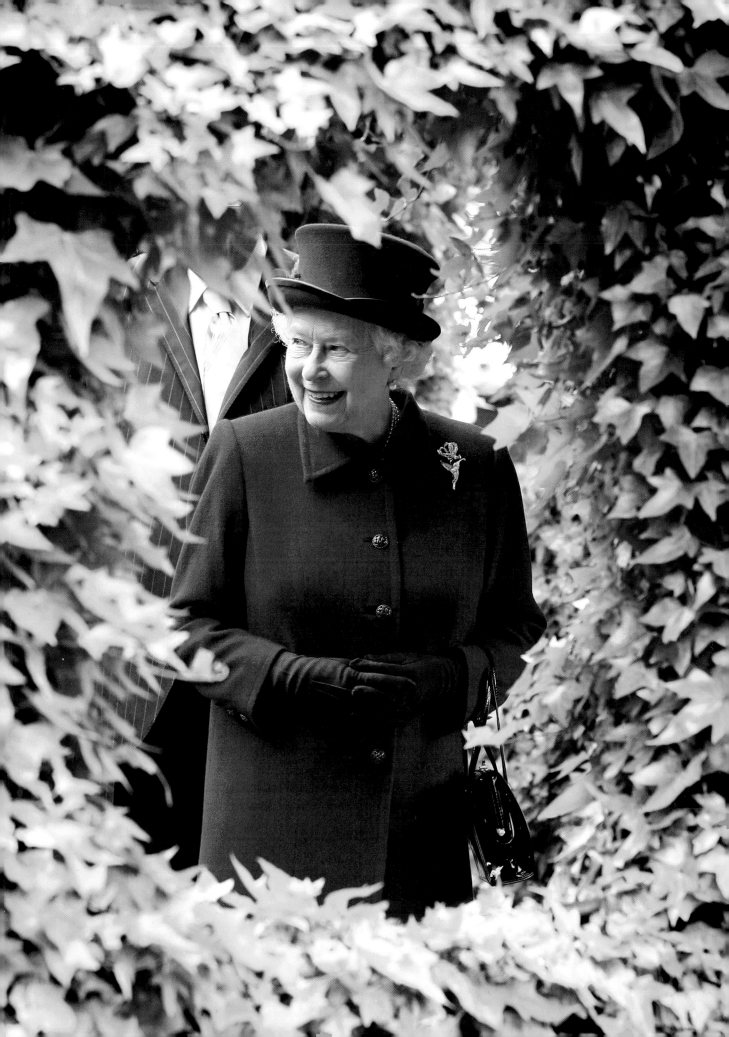

tering it. You must never touch her (although Michelle Obama did, and so far no one has chopped off the First Lady's head). She is severe and slightly scary in the way that people were, once upon a time, when being judgmental was more of a virtue than a vice. She has never given an interview and she never will, because it's not about her. She has a fairy-tale job, but she treats it not as a fantasy but as honest hard work. We all recognize her, we Brits lick the back of her head every time we mail a letter—and yet, after all these years, we hardly know her. She is the Mona Lisa monarch.

Whatever your views on hereditary monarchy, Her Majesty Elizabeth the Second, by the Grace of God, of the United Kingdom of Great Britain and Northern Ireland, and of Her other Realms and Territories, Queen, Head of the Commonwealth, Defender of the Faith, age 86 as of April 21, 2012, is still a force to be reckoned with. So much so that she challenges the prejudices of those who don't believe the monarchy should be allowed to exist at all. As she celebrates her Diamond Jubilee, she has won the grudging respect of some avowed republicans through her sheer stamina and awesome devotion to duty. Even people who hate the monarchy admire the Queen. The argument over whether the United Kingdom should terminate centuries of rule by crowned heads will be revived only after the Queen is gone. Like most Britons, I hope secretly that such a day will never come. Quite simply, we want her to live forever.

It is sixty years since a young woman, almost foal-like with her bright, curious eyes, velvety skin and tremulous energy, was robed in ermine and had St. Edward's crown placed on her head. It was the climax of the coronation in Westminster Abbey, and she made a solemn promise before God to devote her life to her country. Elizabeth was 25 and slight. The crown is old and huge—it includes four gold crosses, 444 precious and semiprecious stones, and weighs 4 lbs., 12 oz. It looked like a candle-snuffer about to obscure the dainty, female head which was doing its solemn best to balance it while the new monarch walked down an aisle. Just to add to the fun, she was being watched by more than 25 million people, who peered at a ghostly black-and-white picture of the first great event of the television age. The establishment was against televising the coronation. Winston Churchill shuddered that the sacred ceremony might be watched "in public houses by men with hats on." Elizabeth put her foot down. And so the new Queen boosted the popularity of a new medium, while the new medium boosted the popularity of the new Queen. It was the first of a thousand shrewd, instinctive decisions.

In the years ahead, the Queen would often be taken for granted because she was modest and rarely made a mistake. She was mocked for being dull—"Duchesses find the Queen dowdy, frumpish and banal," sniffed one snobby critic—and few saw what a brilliant trick it was to make the extraordinary look ordinary.

My generation of women was lucky. We grew up thinking it was perfectly normal to have a female head of state. Although the Queen would be amused to be called a feminist icon, her success as a wise, steadying counsel to twelve Prime Ministers, eleven of them men, has been a great subliminal advert for girl power. In a newspaper column of 1952, shortly after the coronation, one writer argued that "If, as many earnestly pray, the accession of Elizabeth II can help to remove the last shreds of prejudice against women aspiring to the highest places, then a new era for women will indeed be at hand." The columnist's name was Margaret Thatcher.

I witnessed that power myself once, when I got an invitation to a reception for the media at Windsor Castle, back in 2002. Born, like most of my contemporaries, without the deference gene,

I wasn't sure I could make myself drop a curtsy before the sovereign. My resistance was made futile by my 6-year-old daughter, a keen student at the Walt Disney school of princess studies. "Mummy," she said, eyes popping with wonder, "you're going to tea with the Queen. Let's practice curtsying!"

What fun it was to observe the republican media hounds when the Queen entered St. George's Hall that night: all that scorn contorted into embarrassed smiles and tongue-tied schoolboy silences. The mockable could not be mocked close up because, being supremely gentle and dignified, it demanded gentleness and dignity in return. To disarm a pack of journalists was, of course, child's play to someone like the Queen, who has calmed far more restless crowds in her time—not least those who gathered in an angry, mutinous mood outside Buckingham Palace after the tragic early death of Princess Diana, but who simmered down the moment the Queen stepped out of her Rolls-Royce. Then they began to clap.

With her countrywoman's headscarves and her sturdy handbags, the Queen has never been a style setter; but that means she never goes out of fashion. In an age of shameless celebrity, we can rely on her not to fake emotion. "Show Us You Care, Ma'am!" was the belligerent tabloid headline when Diana died and the Queen seemed not to be swayed by the typhoon of public grief. But she has always shown that she cares, by sacrificing herself to her job. At her funeral, they will lay St. Edward's heavy crown on her coffin, and maybe only then will we realize how skillfully that dainty young head of 1952 has carried its great weight for all these years. The one eternal problem that faces Queen Elizabeth II may not be her fault, but it is certainly of her own making, and it will by no means die when she does. It is that she has done her job too well. She is everything a sovereign is meant to be: benign, slightly fierce, inexhaustible, incorruptible and unreadable. She has served her people as honorably as she promised she would at her accession, and possibly rather better than they deserve.

Who on earth can follow such an act? The Prince of Wales is supposed to, but he cannot command a fraction of the loyalty she inspires, and many of his subjects feel that they know too much about him to respect the man, let alone revere him. Also, for some reason the poor chap looks older than his own mum and comes across as spoiled: She has three private secretaries; he has eleven.

Idealists point to the Duke and Duchess of Cambridge, or William and Kate, as they will always be known. The couple's 2011 wedding had so much heart and electricity that we will warm ourselves on its memory for years to come. Could the succession not skip a generation and pass straight from age to youth? The short answer is no. A hereditary monarchy is not a popularity contest. There is a nagging fear that when the Queen finally proves to be mortal, a large measure of the British monarchy will be laid to rest beside her. Some impatient souls in Britain would welcome such a demise, claiming that the country needs to wake up from its fusty monarchical dream. It's a point of view that will, I suspect, utterly bewilder those watching from around the world, since to them, as to most visitors to these shores, Britain *is* the Queen. She is like the weather: always there, overhead, and the cause of our singular constitution. "God save the Queen," her people sing in their national anthem; but history may, in time, reveal a more surprising truth: She saved them.

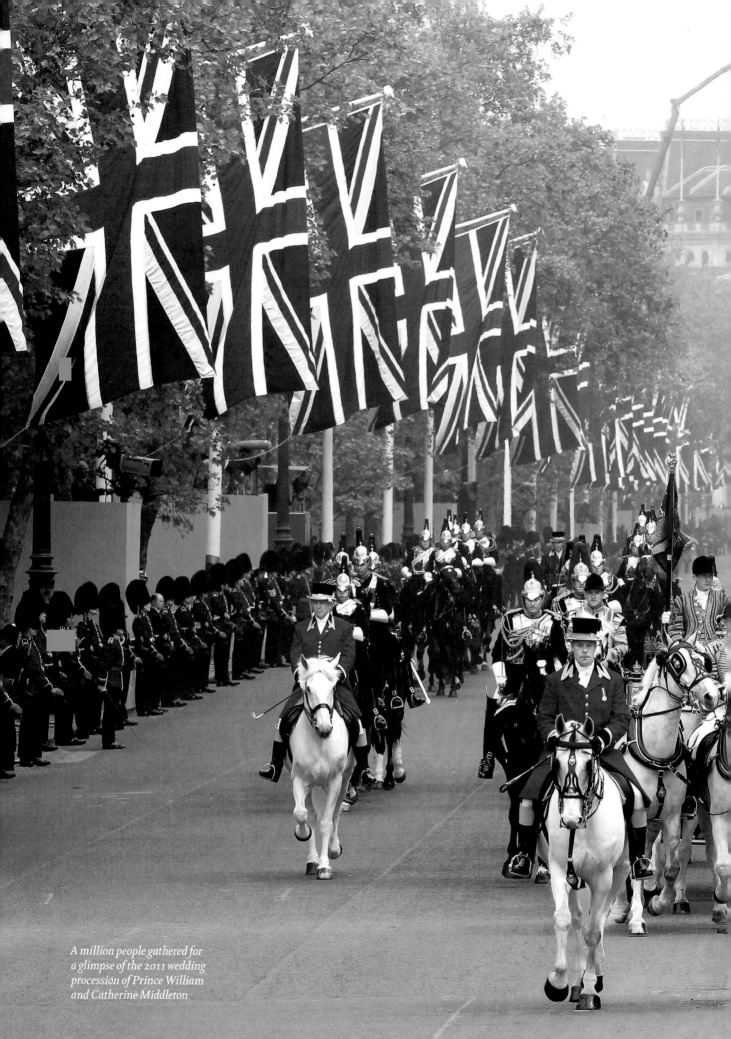

A million people gathered for a glimpse of the 2011 wedding procession of Prince William and Catherine Middleton

They Go Marching On

Governments topple and institutions fail, but Britain's constitutional monarchy maintains its quiet popularity. As the indefatigable Queen celebrates 60 years on the throne, the House of Windsor looks secure, surprisingly so

By Catherine Mayer

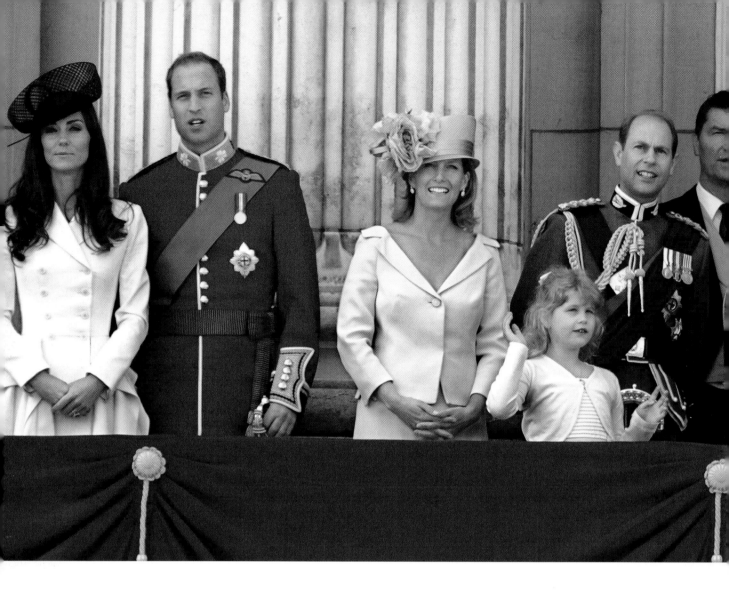

It was a year that drove home one lesson with unusual brutality: Nothing lasts forever, no matter how solid it looks. In 2011 popular anger swept away dictatorial regimes across the Middle East and dysfunctional governments in Europe. The Occupy movement rattled authorities in the U.S. and found raucous echoes around the globe. Fury at austerity budgets sent millions more to the barricades. In London and other parts of England, for five sultry nights, there were riots. From Athens to Moscow, one impulse, often inchoate, brought people onto the street: to wrest power from institutions.

Yet in the midst of all that, the United Kingdom's biggest demonstration of popular opinion, on April 29, indicated that at least one institution still commanded wide respect. In the chill of predawn, crowds converged on the capital to participate in an event

Catherine Mayer is TIME's *Europe editor*

that promised to be a piece of history. These people, a million or more, came not in anger but in optimism, to cheer an ancient organization putting on the pomp to observe a traditional rite. They came to celebrate the wedding of Prince William Arthur Philip Louis, the second-in-line to the British throne, to Catherine Elizabeth Middleton, a commoner elevated through their marriage to Duchess of Cambridge and to a leading position to become, one day, Queen.

The royal wedding, and the celebration in 2012 of Elizabeth II's Diamond Jubilee, her 60th year on the throne, mark something of a comeback for the Windsor dynasty, which just 20 years ago appeared irretrievably tainted by scandal and divorce. Things looked as if they couldn't get worse, but they did, in 1997, with the death of Princess Diana. For the royals, however, comebacks run in the family. The most extraordinary characteristic of the extraordinary phenomenon that is Britain's monarchy is its ability to endure and renew. Since Charles II was installed

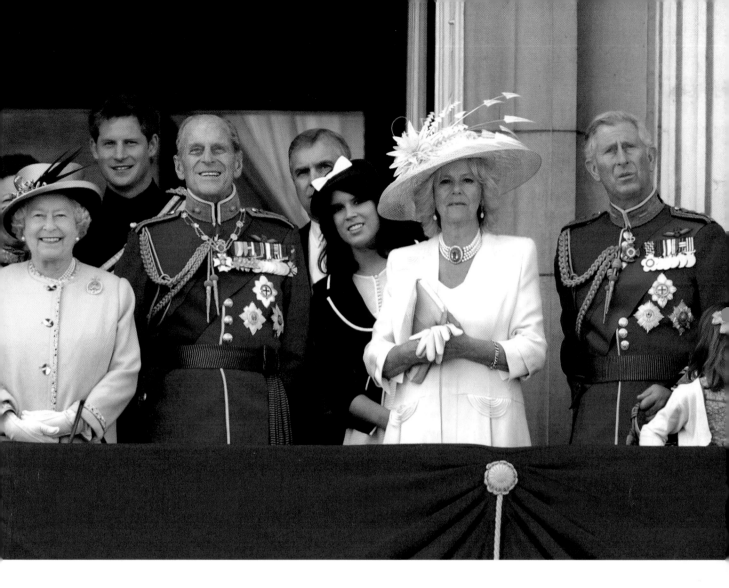

From left, on the balcony of Buckingham Palace for the June 2011 Trooping of the Colour ceremony: Catherine, Duchess of Cambridge; Prince William; Sophie, Countess of Wessex; Lady Louise Windsor; Prince Edward; Sir Timothy Laurence; Princess Anne; Queen Elizabeth II; Prince Harry; Prince Philip; Prince Andrew; Princess Eugenie; Camilla, Duchess of Cornwall; Prince Charles

on the throne in 1660, at the end of an 11-year experiment in republicanism that started with the decapitation of his father on the orders of Parliament, kings and queens have kept their heads and acted as heads of state. Their survival has relied on a willingness to adapt to public opinion without fatally undermining the idea that royals are different from most folk—for the people, yet above the people.

No monarch has faced down greater existential challenges or perfected the technique of quiet adjustment to shifting realities with greater skill than the current Queen. The throngs that packed central London to see her grandson and his bride may have been caught up in the romance of a story sprinkled with the residual stardust of the groom's iconic mother and the fairy-tale plot line of a nice but ordinary girl snaring a prince; but they would not have turned up at all if not for the Queen's achievement in navigating more than half a century of tumult.

Her Diamond Jubilee year opened with no letup

in the popular unrest that in the previous year had dismantled seemingly impregnable establishments. The United Kingdom itself could be imperiled as Scottish nationalists look forward to a 2014 referendum on independence. Yet those same nationalists have pledged to keep Elizabeth II as head of state whatever the outcome of the vote, and there are festivities planned on both sides of the border to mark the Queen's Jubilee. During an extended holiday weekend in June, the focus will return to London with a flotilla of 1,000 boats expected to accompany the sovereign's barge along the Thames, a concert at the gates of Buckingham Palace, a carriage

13

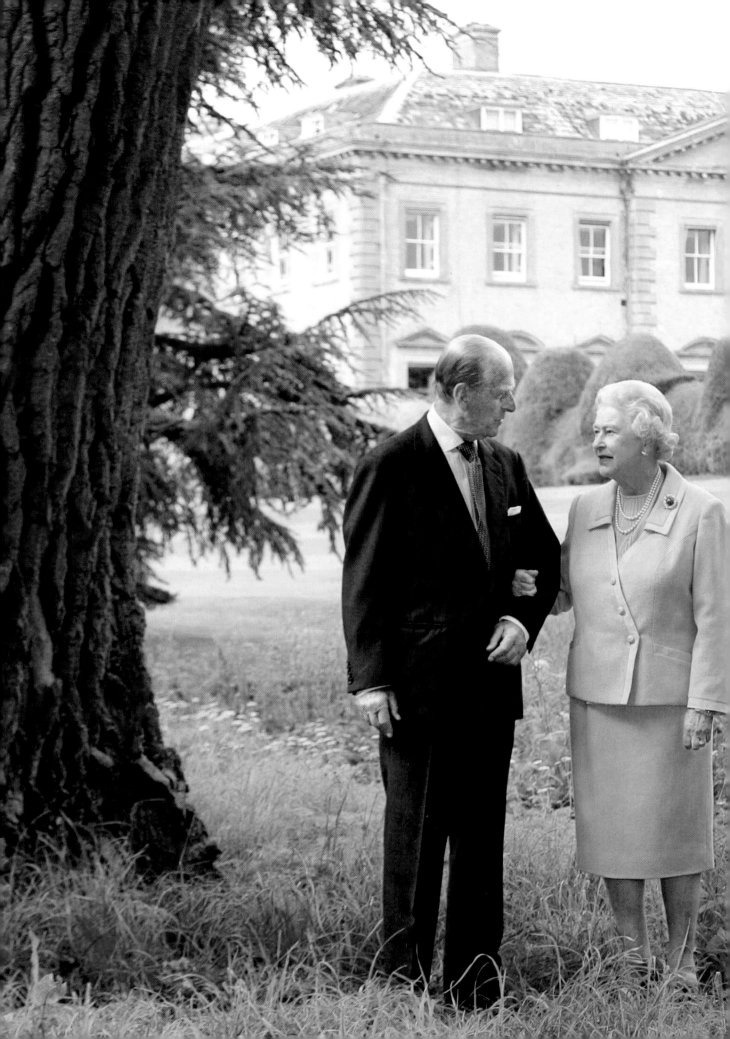

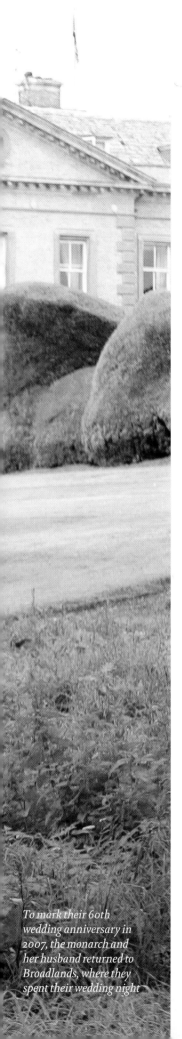

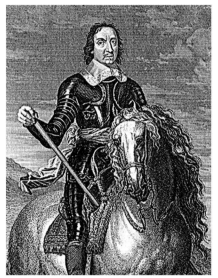

Oliver Cromwell led the short-lived republic until his death in 1658

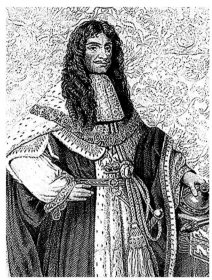

In 1660 the monarchy was restored, and Charles II returned from his European exile

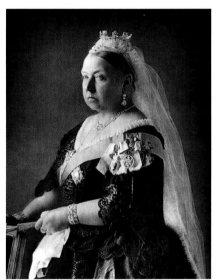

Queen Victoria reigned for 64 years, longer than any other British monarch

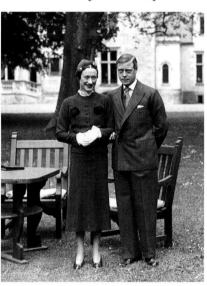

The Duke of Windsor and Wallis Simpson toured France in 1937 after his abdication

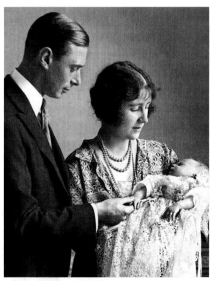

When Princess Elizabeth was born, her parents didn't expect her to ascend the throne

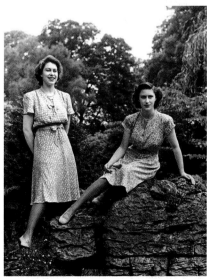

Young Elizabeth (left) and her sister, Margaret, at Windsor Great Park in 1946

procession to a thanksgiving service at St. Paul's Cathedral and, in an oddly sci-fi touch, the Queen will trigger a giant laser to light the last in a series of beacons to be illuminated across the U.K.

Britain's anti-monarchists—and there are more than a few, around a fifth of Britons, according to polls, with 20,000 of them signed up as supporters of the pressure group Republic—are preparing to celebrate too. For them the Jubilee presages the beginning of the end of the Elizabethan age and the eventual transition to a less sure-footed monarch.

In 1936, the monarchy survived the abdication of Edward VIII, who gave up the throne to marry the American divorcée Wallis Simpson. Indeed, the monarchy emerged stronger for it. That says something about where the two biggest risks to the institution reside: Any crisis raises questions about its continued existence, and it is only as good as its leader. King George VI, Edward's successor, stilled the questions raised by the abdication by proving far better suited to the kingship than his capricius brother, courageously overcoming his famous stammer to articulate a vision of national unity in a time of war. His daughter Elizabeth II has only rarely put a foot wrong. Her son and heir, the Prince of Wales, has not always appeared so deft.

So republicans see in the beacons lit to celebrate the Queen's Jubilee the flames that may one day consume the monarchy. That ignores the institution's resilience. To understand why it has endured, one must understand what it has endured, and how it has anchored itself at the heart of British life. Because the people who plan to congregate on that Jubilee weekend—those who will wave flags and strain for a glimpse of the Queen's famous wave—agree on one issue with the people planning to protest the festivities: Like it or not, the monarchy still matters.

If 60 years doesn't seem like much in the sweep of human history, it's worth listening to a BBC radio report filed from Kenya on the day Princess Elizabeth became Queen. She was traveling there with her husband, the Duke of Edinburgh (she didn't make Philip a prince until 1957). The journalist Frank Gillard, who covered the royal visit, spoke with the distinctive upper-crust accent, A's shortened into E's, that has come to be called the Queen's English. Gillard recounted that he had seen Elizabeth shortly after 9

o'clock in the morning. "Then, looking a little tired but very heppy, she was driving away from the Treetops hut where she and the duke had spent the previous 19 hours, about as far removed from normal civilization as possible, even in Efrica." Her heppiness would last until news of her father's sudden death could be communicated by telegram and trunk calls and she learned of her loss—and her gain in status. "In the words of a member of the household," intoned Gillard, "she bore it like a Queen."

Six decades later, the Queen's subjects not only talk in different accents, the terms of their conversations have changed. Technology has been a key driver of that change, speeding communications and, in a foreshadowing of today's protest movements, breaking the stranglehold of big institutions like the BBC or Buckingham Palace on those communications and redrawing their terms of engagement. Journalists have long ceased to defer to the establishment. Before the end of the 20th century, a pack of paparazzi pursued Diana, Princess of Wales, into the Pont de l'Alma tunnel in Paris with tragic consequences. The disclosure in 2006 that the royal editor of the British Sunday tabloid *News of the World,* together with a private investigator on the newspaper's payroll, had hacked into the voicemail of Princes William and Harry made clear that the Windsors were considered fair game by the media, to be treated no better than garden-variety celebrities. The public evidently agreed. The hacking scandal would eventually bring down the 186-year-old tabloid (another seemingly impregnable institution to bite the dust in 2011), but only after it emerged that ordinary people, including victims of crime, had been targeted. Nobody seemed to worry too much about the rights of the Windsors to a private life.

That wasn't just because Britain and the wider world had become less deferential, though they had. The monarchy could no longer assume that anyone would bend the knee. When Princess Elizabeth was born, the British Empire extended across a quarter of the planet. By the time she ascended the throne, former colonies were asserting their independence. Then came the social revolutions of the 1960s, enshrining teenage rebellion against authority not as a passing phase but as a way of life and vaunting peace and love over the more traditional virtues embodied by the royals, like responsibility and duty. By the time of the Queen's Silver Jubilee, in 1977, the idealism of the previous decade had curdled into something more confrontational. "God save the Queen/She ain't no human being," intoned the Sex Pistols. Remote as Britain's head of state was, those words resonated.

They did so because another societal shift had altered expectations: the erosion of the private sphere. Everyone, even uptight Brits, had been learning by degrees to let it all hang out. Therapy culture fused with celebrity culture. People now expected to know everything about everyone. The Queen made concessions; she developed the walkabout, braving direct contact with crowds and reportedly joking, "To see me is to believe me." She broadened the old guest lists for palace entertainment from the posh and privileged to a more diversified representation of British life. She sometimes allowed TV cameras through her doors. But she remained, by instinct, a private person.

Those instincts were largely sound. The Queen is at least as famous as any celebrity on the planet, but she is beyond mere familiarity. She has preserved the sense of difference necessary to retain the support and respect of four-fifths of Britons and majorities in the 15 other countries where she serves as head of state and to hold together the Commonwealth of Nations.

The benefits to the countries that maintain a link to the Crown are hard to quantify. That does not mean they do not exist. A relationship with the Queen, at least in some eyes, still confers status and enhances national cohesion. "Monarchy is extremely important to this country," Prime Minister David Cameron told TIME. "It's a reminder of our history and a symbol of national pride. But above all, it's important because right at the top of British life we have this institution that is nonpolitical, that isn't subject to the winds of change. That gives a certain strength and stability to this country, that people of all parties and none have an institution they can admire and feel proud of."

The Queen may have her Prime Minister's vote, but she works hard to steer clear of anything that could be construed as party politics. The body of conventions that combine to create Britain's unwritten constitution demand of the monarch a scrupulous neutrality that can be tested if she is called on to perform another of her duties and appoint a Prime Minister. Usually she rubber-stamps the voters' or parties' choice, but the sudden resignation in 1957 of Prime Minister Anthony Eden and a subsequent stalemate over his replacement created a problem. She followed the advice of senior politicians in appointing his successor but attracted criticism from supporters of the unsuccessful candidate. More recently, in May 2010, when parliamentary elections failed to produce a clear majority, the Queen stood back and waited for the parties concerned to reach a resolution. Five days after polling stations closed, Cameron traveled to Buckingham Palace so the Queen could officially appoint him to lead the coalition government the politicians had hammered out without her intervention.

That does not mean the monarchy has no role in the transition from one government to the next. The monarchy provides a symbol of stability and continuity at just such times, says Dr. Richard Chartres, the bishop of London; it is "the element in the constitution that is beyond partisanship." Chartres, a royal advisor and family friend who led the funeral service for Princess Diana and gave the sermon at the wedding of William and Kate, asserts that royalty is at the core of British life: "Our head of state stands for common human values, exemplifies the life we all know. And the fact that the focus of unity is someone without raw political power but exemplifying those values has a considerable impact on the life of the community at every level, because people are brought to see that there is a realm beyond the clash of ideas and programs. And that humanizes a society."

The millions of people who lined the route to Westminster Abbey for William and Kate's wedding or Diana's funeral and the millions more who will celebrate the Queen's Diamond Jubilee may not express in such high-flown terms the reasons they consider these events worth marking. Some will say they like the Queen. Others might talk about Kate's beauty and Diana's, or their emotional connection to figures most of them have never met. A smaller number will grouch about them. Everyone has different reactions to the royal family, but nobody fails to have an opinion. In a world of constant change, the House of Windsor stands out, a familiar, fascinating landmark.

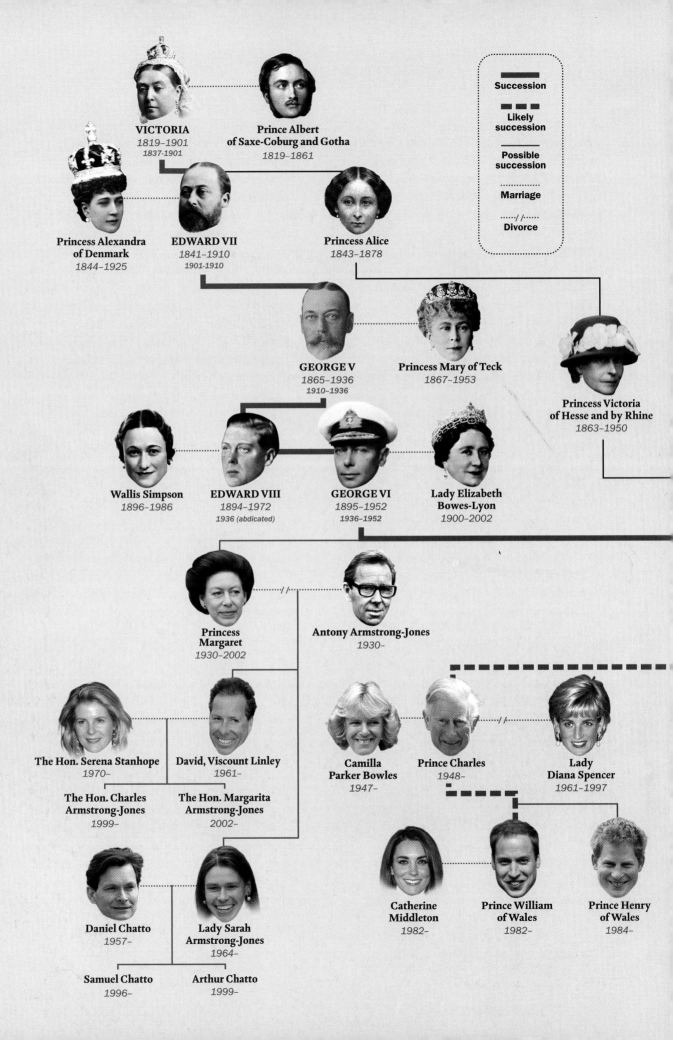

VICTORIA
1819–1901
1837-1901

Prince Albert
of Saxe-Coburg and Gotha
1819–1861

Princess Alexandra
of Denmark
1844–1925

EDWARD VII
1841–1910
1901-1910

Princess Alice
1843–1878

Succession

Likely succession

Possible succession

Marriage

Divorce

GEORGE V
1865–1936
1910–1936

Princess Mary of Teck
1867–1953

Princess Victoria
of Hesse and by Rhine
1863–1950

Wallis Simpson
1896–1986

EDWARD VIII
1894–1972
1936 (abdicated)

GEORGE VI
1895–1952
1936–1952

Lady Elizabeth
Bowes-Lyon
1900–2002

Princess Margaret
1930–2002

Antony Armstrong-Jones
1930–

The Hon. Serena Stanhope
1970–

David, Viscount Linley
1961–

Camilla Parker Bowles
1947–

Prince Charles
1948–

Lady Diana Spencer
1961–1997

The Hon. Charles
Armstrong-Jones
1999–

The Hon. Margarita
Armstrong-Jones
2002–

Catherine Middleton
1982–

Prince William of Wales
1982–

Prince Henry of Wales
1984–

Daniel Chatto
1957–

Lady Sarah
Armstrong-Jones
1964–

Samuel Chatto
1996–

Arthur Chatto
1999–

From Victoria to the Windsors

This simplified family tree traces the main line of succession from Queen Victoria through the current Queen and on to her heirs. This does not represent a complete picture of the family or of the complex skein of relationships created by the royal habit of marrying cousins. Elizabeth II and Prince Philip, for example, are both descended from Queen Victoria. The Windsor name was first adopted by George V during World War I, to replace the family's original—and indisputably German—surname, Saxe-Coburg and Gotha. The Battenbergs became the Mountbattens during the same period.

Graphic by Lon Tweeten

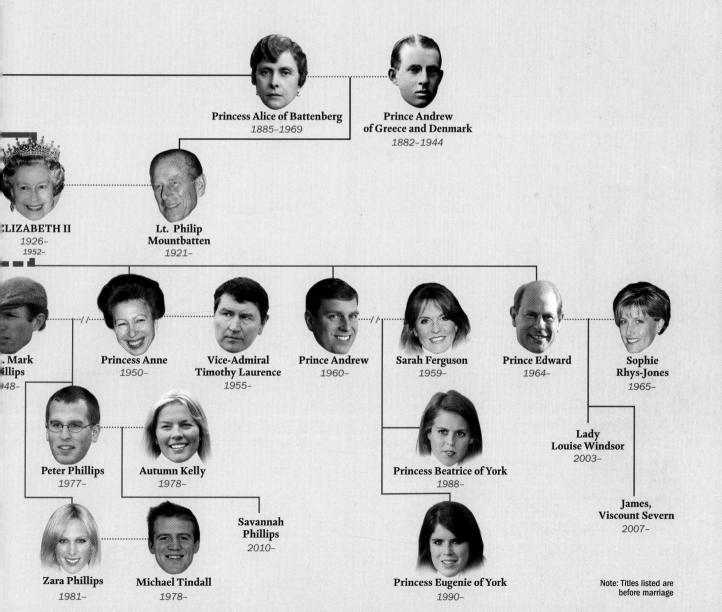

Princess Alice of Battenberg
1885–1969

Prince Andrew of Greece and Denmark
1882–1944

ELIZABETH II
1926–
1952–

Lt. Philip Mountbatten
1921–

. Mark ₁illips
₀48–

Princess Anne
1950–

Vice-Admiral Timothy Laurence
1955–

Prince Andrew
1960–

Sarah Ferguson
1959–

Prince Edward
1964–

Sophie Rhys-Jones
1965–

Peter Phillips
1977–

Autumn Kelly
1978–

Princess Beatrice of York
1988–

Lady Louise Windsor
2003–

Savannah Phillips
2010–

James, Viscount Severn
2007–

Zara Phillips
1981–

Michael Tindall
1978–

Princess Eugenie of York
1990–

Note: Titles listed are before marriage

The Head That Wears The Crown

She's shrewd and strategic, funny and fearsome. She has the skills to run a multinational. Meet the unseen Queen

By Catherine Mayer

You sense her approach before you see her. There's a straightening of shoulders among palace staff, a determined clip of shoes on polished floors, and another sound, harder to place, like autumn leaves blown across tarmac. Then a pack of corgis and dorgis—dachshunds crossed with corgis—comes skittering into view, as many as six, their nails percussive on the sections of parquet not muted by rugs as they surge ahead of their diminutive owner.

One of the first things people notice about the Queen is how closely she fits their expectations, whether she is accompanied by a retinue of corgis or of courtiers, is dressed down in dowdy daywear or gussied up in silks and tiara. The second is how tiny she is. Famous people often surprise us in the flesh— they turn out to be more imposing than we imagined, or less so; prove warmer than their public image, or spikier. Today's second-longest-serving monarch (after Thailand's current king) may look far too petite to shoulder her extraordinary mass of accrued experience and global celebrity. Yet in other respects she is exactly as we imagine her: regal and serious-minded, familiar yet enigmatic. Her second son, Prince Andrew, tells a story of his mother on a stroll encountering one of her subjects, who exclaimed, "You look just like the Queen!" "How reassuring," the Queen replied—two words that could serve as the perfect epigraph for her 60-year reign.

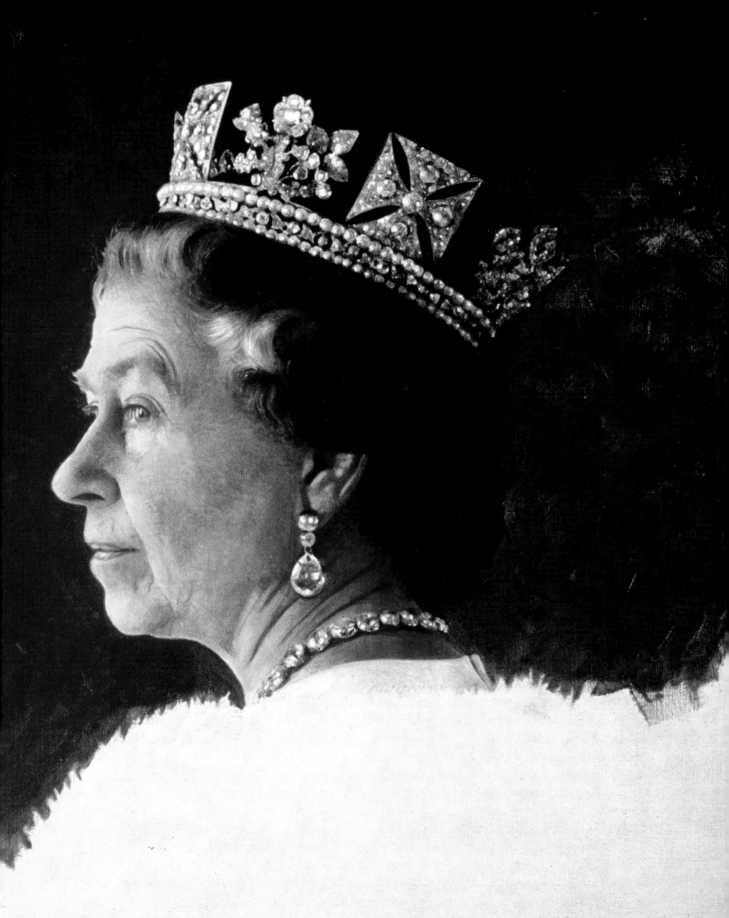

She isn't just a symbolic figure. The Queen also runs one of the world's best-known brands

Few of us remember a world without Elizabeth II. She represents consistency; she embodies tradition. We've heard her speak, many times, but she gives us little insight into what she really thinks. Other members of her family have at times visibly struggled with the burden of balancing their private impulses with their public status. The Queen's demeanor has never cracked. When she has attracted criticism, it has not been for what she has said or done, but for her reticence.

The great 19th-century essayist Walter Bagehot wrote of the monarchy, "Its mystery is its life. We must not let in daylight upon magic," and this precept still holds, perhaps more so than ever in an age of disposable celebrity. The Queen does not make herself available for interviews and has no intention of ever doing so. Her enduring popularity—and the longer-term survival of the constitutional monarchy—rests on a notion rarely articulated in our egalitarian times: that she and her heirs are special, different, above the hoi polloi. In at least some respects, that otherness isn't just a notion. On closer observation, the Windsors, especially the monarch's generation and her children's, turn out to be quite unlike most Britons much less the peoples of the further-flung Commonwealth realms that still bend the knee to Elizabeth II. The rarified environment the royals inhabit makes them see things differently—and sometimes not at all. Prince Andrew, on a visit to China in 2004, told students at Beijing University that U.S. culture had exerted little influence on British culture. The students looked back at him, bemused, perhaps more aware than their English visitor of how American TV, pop music and fashion have shaped the tastes and cultural output of his country for generations. The royals' upbringing means they do not always naturally connect with the people they are taught from infancy they are born to serve. But connect with them they must.

Only rarely has the Queen badly misjudged public sentiment. In 1966 she was criticized for being remote and out of touch when she did not rush straight to the South Wales town of Aberfan after a landslide of coal waste buried a school, killing 116 children and 28 adults. She drew negative comment again for missing the funeral of 10-year-old Joanne Flannigan, the first service for a local victim of the 1988 downing of Pan Am Flight 103 over the Scot-

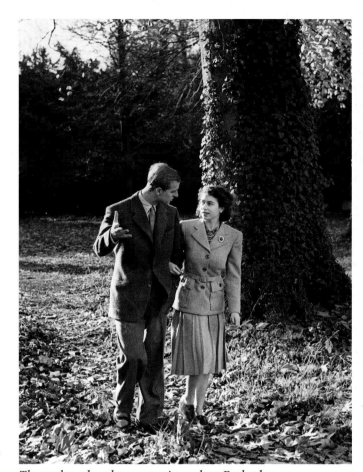

The royal couple on honeymoon in southern England, 1947

tish town of Lockerbie. "Broken-hearted Britain watching TV needed to see their equally grieving monarch," wrote columnist Jean Rook in the *Daily Express.* The movie *The Queen* dramatized the sovereign's most serious misstep of all, when she delayed her return to London to lead the national mourning after the 1997 death of her former daughter-in-law.

These were mistakes Diana herself would never have made. Though a child of the aristocracy, the Princess was plugged into the demotic, democratic world outside the palace gates. She grasped, as she told Martin Bashir in her startlingly revelatory 1995 TV interview, that "knowledge is power." The knowledge she deployed to seduce the populace and bind them to her, however, was not the content of the detailed briefs aides routinely prepare for royals ahead of public engagements, but emotional intelligence. Diana's told her that while sharing pain publicly may or may not help to ease it, such displays are the currency of modern celebrity. To the Queen, raised to keep a poker face and a stiff

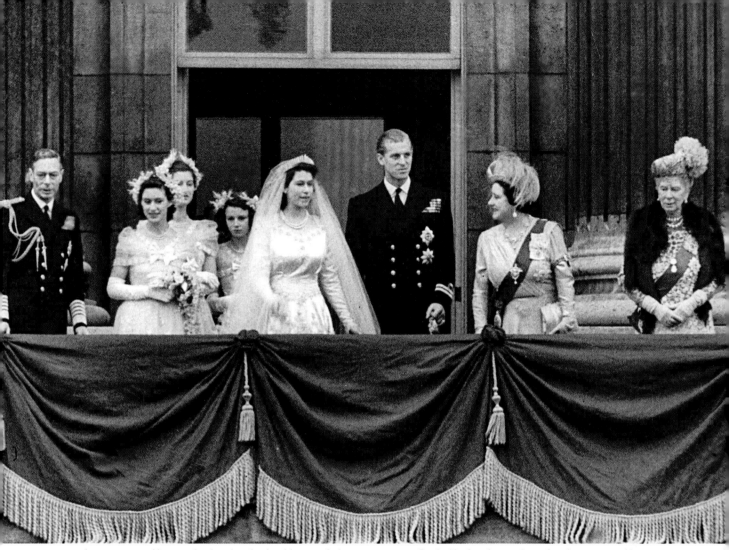

The Princess and her new husband make the obligatory balcony appearance flanked by family members after their 1947 wedding

upper lip and never to let down her guard in front of the servants much less in front of TV cameras, Diana's behavior must have seemed as foreign as any of the 129 countries the Queen has visited during her reign.

The social and cultural landscapes of her own nation surely seem increasingly alien too. Britain's infamously sclerotic class system lingers, but the deference it once commanded has long since evaporated. Social mores have changed: At the start of her reign, divorcées were excluded from court functions, a stigma that dissuaded the Queen's sister, Princess Margaret, from marrying a divorced suitor. But by 1992, 11% of British unions were ending in divorce, and by 1996, 75% of the monarch's children's first marriages had been dissolved. (The national rate threatened to catch up but is again declining as fewer people bother to get married.) Republicanism remains a minority interest, but even ardent royalists sometimes struggle to articulate what the Queen does beyond acting as a living tourist attraction and lending her image to coinage and stamps.

As celebrations for the Diamond Jubilee encourage us to look back over the second Elizabethan era, it is tempting to see the monarchy and its matriarch as relics, preserved in a sticky aspic of nostalgia and sentiment. That would be to underestimate an institution that, against all odds, is quietly thriving and a sovereign who, at 86, is more influential than for many a decade. Her leadership has steered the monarchy through crises and social upheaval. She has built an organization highly skilled at change management. And now it is preparing for the biggest change it will ever have to manage: one day to manage without her.

The Figurehead Is Not What She Seems

To spend time around the Queen is to appreciate how easy it is even for those closest to her to ignore the passing years. Aides half her age complain of exhaustion after attempting—and failing—to keep pace with her on overseas trips. She has barely

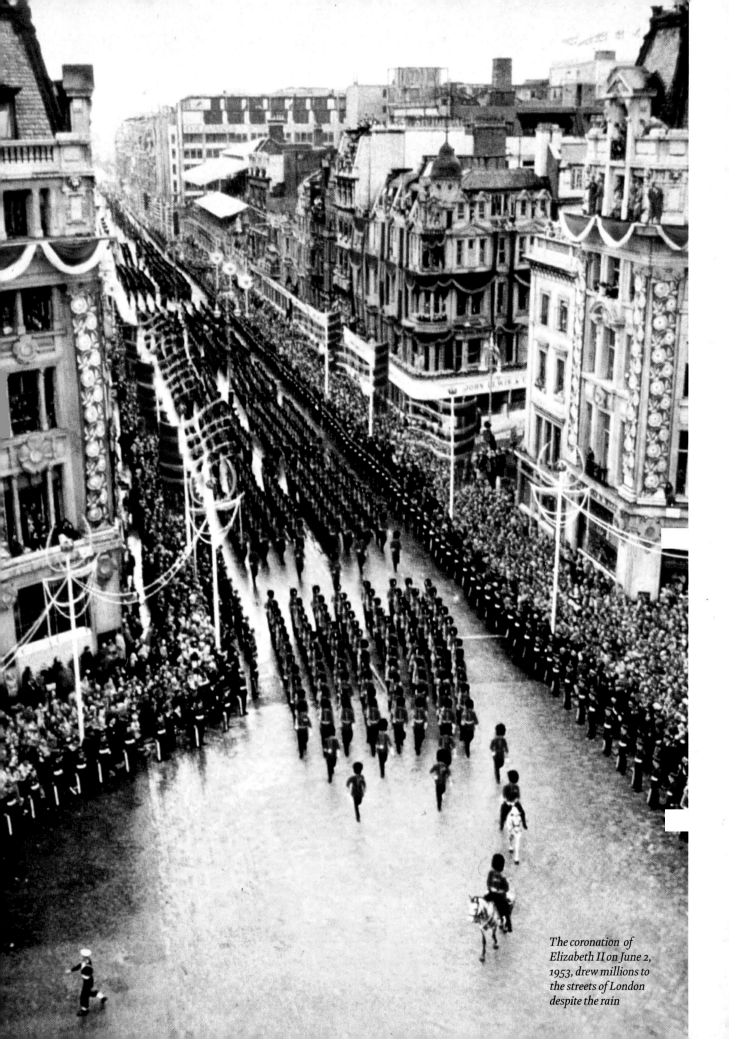

The coronation of Elizabeth II on June 2, 1953, drew millions to the streets of London despite the rain

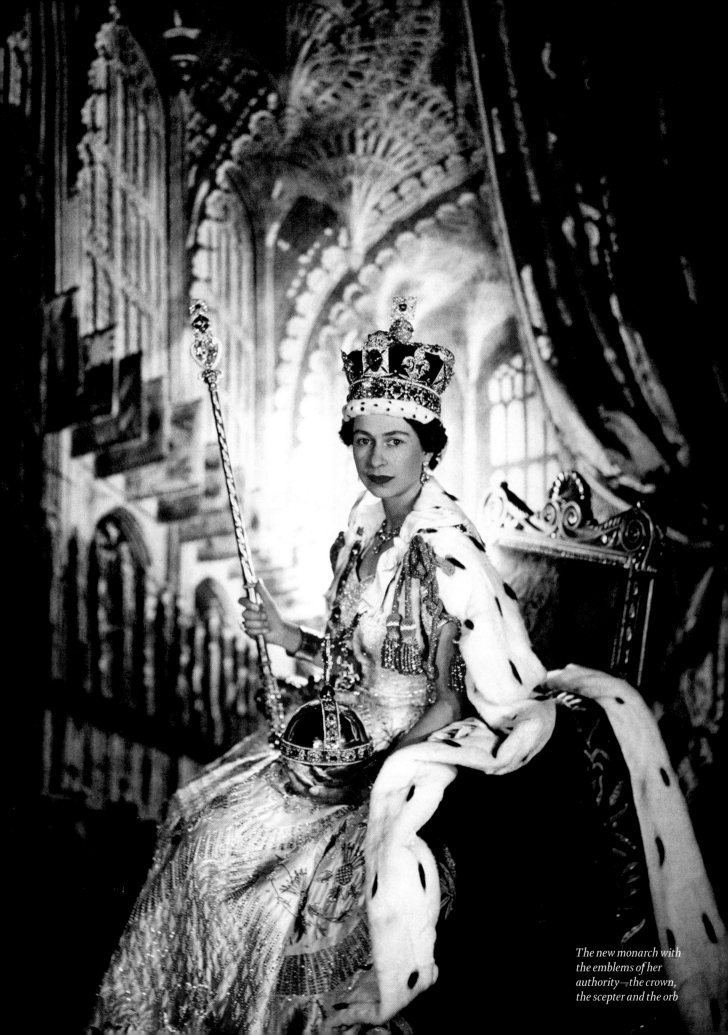

trimmed her workload since her 1977 Silver Jubilee. In 2011 her toll of engagements—which included action-packed state visits to Ireland and Australia and hosting the Obamas for a three-day visit—actually rose by 20% over the previous year. The Diamond Jubilee will see her traverse Britain, Prince Philip in tow. The only other queen—and the only other British monarch—to last 60 years on the throne was Queen Victoria, and by the time of that milestone, she was too infirm to leave her carriage to attend the thanksgiving service inside St. Paul's Cathedral, forcing clerics to move the ceremony to the roadside instead. Elizabeth II intends to walk cathedral aisles

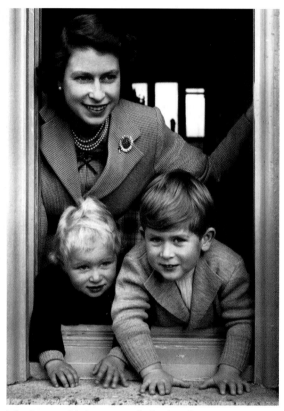

The Queen with Anne, 2, and Charles, almost 4, in 1952

and rope-line miles and clamber on and off boats and trains during her Jubilee year.

Though the Queen herself may seem ageless, there are aspects of Palace life that positively creak. Honorary positions at court still include an official called the earl marshal, charged with arranging the sovereign's funeral and overseeing the coronation of the sovereign's successor. The title, which passes to each successive Duke of Norfolk and is now held by the 18th, is a hangover from the days when mon-

archs relied on the nobility to manage their affairs. There's also an astronomer royal, the Queen's piper, royal watermen, ladies of the bedchamber and the crown equerry. Watching 12 bagpipers process around the crystal-laden table at a state banquet or noticing that most of the British women attending have accessorized their evening gowns with sashes and family jewels reinforces the notion that Buckingham Palace is only that—a palace, a living museum. In fact it is the corporate headquarters of one of the world's best-known brands and one of the pillars of Britain's unwritten constitution. Look past the footmen and valets and flummery, and one finds an organization run at least as professionally as many multinationals.

That hasn't always been true. Until the 1990s, the household consisted mostly of retired military personnel, superannuated diplomats and gentry. As the Palace has modernized, some jobs have retained historic titles—the monarchy's chief financial officer is still called the keeper of the privy purse; the royal event organizers, surely the Rolls-Royces of party planners, work out of the lord chamberlain's office—but the Queen's 1,200 paid staff are selected on merit, not bloodline.

As for the boss, she did inherit her job, but she's a natural. The Queen "would make a good CEO," says one official. "Though she is interested in the details, she doesn't get into the weeds." Prime Minister David Cameron agrees: "A vital skill for a CEO is the ability to see the bigger picture, and she's certainly got that. I see her once a week to discuss the issues of the day, and I've noticed her knack for placing them in the broad sweep of events. Perhaps that's what 60 years in the job gives you."

The Queen has indeed spent long years in the university of life. But the more you know about her early life, the more you wonder at her smarts and steeliness. Her education was entrusted to governesses and a series of ad hoc tutors, albeit of lofty pedigree. (After her father, much to his surprise, became King, he gave her a crash course in constitutional matters; she learned about religion from the Archbishop of Canterbury.) Her resilience and grace under pressure probably come from her redoubtable mother, a Scottish aristocrat born Elizabeth Bowes-Lyon, who won admiration for her determination to remain in Buckingham Palace

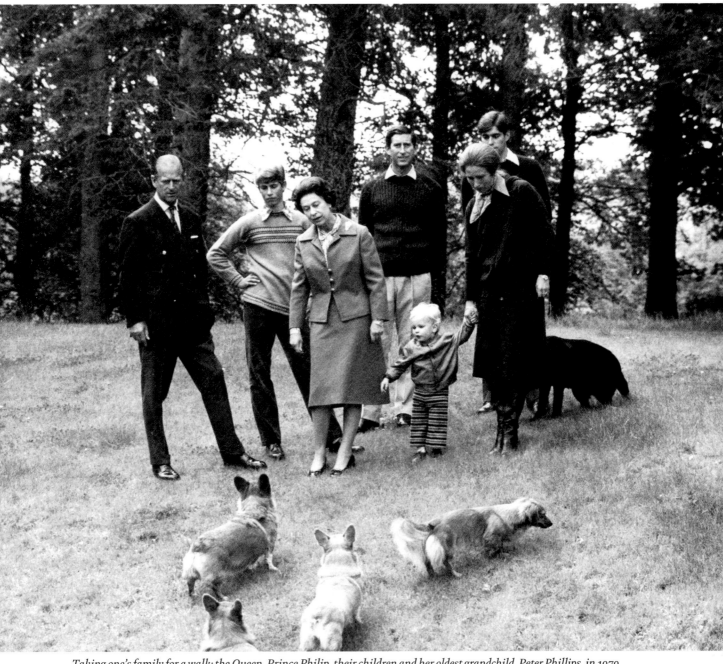

Taking one's family for a walk: the Queen, Prince Philip, their children and her oldest grandchild, Peter Phillips, in 1979

during the Blitz, against the urgings of her advisors. "The children won't go without me," she said. "I won't leave the King. And the King will never leave." In the end, her children spent much of the war at Windsor Castle, just outside the capital. German bombers scored seven separate direct hits on Buckingham Palace, and Princess Elizabeth caught more than an inkling of what she described in her 21st-birthday address, from Cape Town, as the "terrible and glorious years" of World War II.

In that same 1947 speech, the future Queen enunciated the twin-track mission that would define her life. She told radio listeners across the British Empire, "I declare before you all that my whole life, whether it be long or short, shall be devoted to your service and to the service of our great imperial family to which we all belong." By the time Elizabeth II ascended the throne, that imperial family was shrinking, as former colonies cast off British rule, many opting for Commonwealth membership

The Prince Consort

By Howard Chua-Eoan

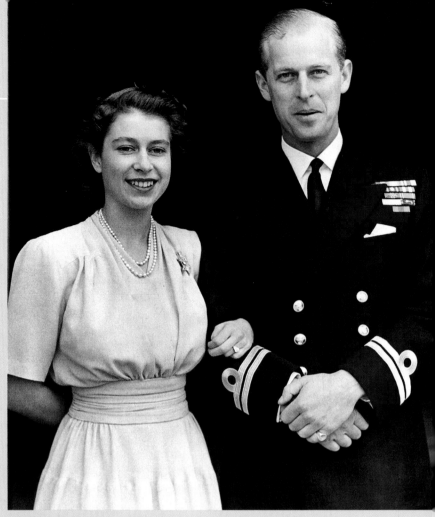

Princess Elizabeth and Lt. Philip Mountbatten in 1947, recently engaged

Being married to the British sovereign is a feat of immense ego suppression. Prince Philip is always one step behind the Queen, always defers to her in public. For the first five years of their marriage, he was the Duke of Edinburgh and the official head of the family. Indeed, until her accession, she was officially the Duchess of Edinburgh. But then she became Queen, and everything was hers—Her Majesty's this; Her Majesty's that; Her Majesty's mark here, there and everywhere. It was not easy being the duke. In 2011, asked by the BBC about his role as the Queen's Silver Jubilee approached, he said, "Constitutionally, I don't exist."

He was a particularly rootless young nobleman, always searching for stability. If anyone was ever a princely pauper, it was Philip Schleswig-Holstein-Sonderburg-Glücksburg. He was born in 1921 atop a kitchen table on the island of Corfu in the Ionian Sea. His father, Andrew, was a ne'er-do-well gambler, the seventh son of a Danish prince who had been plucked out of Scandinavia to become king of Greece, the uneasiest of crowns. His mother, Alice, was practically deaf and communicated via sign language. She was a Battenberg, a British family of German origin that changed its surname to Mountbatten during World War I, about the same time the British Royal Family opted to become the Windsors instead of the Saxe-Coburg-Gothas. In public, Philip was styled Prince Philip of Greece and Denmark. But as his parents' marriage disintegrated, he lived as an exile all over the place, in Paris, in England, in Germany, in Scotland. In 1992, when an interviewer asked him what language he spoke at home, he responded, "What do you mean by 'at home'?"

At the age of 18, however, Philip of Greece was the strikingly handsome guide who took Princess Elizabeth and her sister, Princess Margaret, on a tour of his naval college in Britain in 1939. Elizabeth was infatuated. During World War II she kept his photograph on her dressing table, even though her father didn't quite approve; Philip wasn't really from the right side of the royal track (though he and Elizabeth shared Queen Victoria as a great-great-great grandmother). Philip had to renounce any loyalty to Greece and its soon-to-be-deposed royals. He also had to choose communion with the Church of England instead of the Greek Orthodox. But as soon as those matters were settled, the couple were wed in spectacular style in November 1947. Five years later, she was Queen. She made her husband Prince Philip, Duke of Edinburgh, in 1957.

Her early reign was not accompanied by marital bliss. Philip wanted the dynasty to change its name to Mountbatten-Windsor. His wife would not hear of it. Furious, Philip said, "I'm just a bloody amoeba! That's all." Eventually, a compromise was reached: Grandchildren who did not qualify for the designation "royal highness" would take the hyphenated surname. In a tribute to her father, the Princess Royal Anne, Philip's favorite child, signed "Mountbatten-Windsor" on the registry when she married in 1973.

The years seemed to mellow Philip somewhat, though he had difficulty concealing his disapproval of his son Charles. He was also given to gaffes and the more-than-occasional discordant quote. Visiting China, he told a group of British students that "if you stay here much longer, you'll all be slitty-eyed"; in Scotland, he asked a driving instructor, "How do you keep the natives off the booze long enough to get them through the test?" And an unmistakably English guest at a state banquet for the Mexican president was amused to be hailed by Philip in the receiving line with the words, "Thank heavens, one of us."

Philip and Elizabeth exude palpable affection when they're seen in public together, and in unguarded moments, the usually austere Queen is, in the word of one observer, "kittenish" with her husband. Yet they live apart more often than otherwise. They occupy different bedrooms in Buckingham Palace and other royal residences. The only bed they share is in Balmoral, an estate he helps manage. He dislikes her corgis. They do not regularly speak in the morning. Their private secretaries coordinate their schedules. If they dine together in London, they part ways after the meal, he to read, she to watch television. He likes sailing, a reminder of the promising naval career he gave up when he married.

When Philip speaks of his wife to others, he too refers to her as "the Queen." But when they speak to each other, he still calls her by her childhood nickname, Lilibet, a term of endearment from their early years, before she became the Queen and he became the ceremonial royal consort.

instead. The Queen, now head of the Commonwealth, handled the transition with the unblinking ease of someone schooled by war to appreciate the impermanence of even the most solid-looking edifices. That same sensibility has also enabled her to understand that while Britons consent to the monarchy now, they may not do so in future.

The turbulence of 1992 reinforced that point. Her two older sons' marriages failed, and Britons struggling through an economic downturn wondered why their taxes were subsidizing feckless royals. A fire at Windsor Castle set the seal on what she termed her "*annus horribilis*." In a speech at a banquet marking the 40th anniversary of her accession, she remarked with a touch of acidity familiar to those who know her, "I daresay that history will take a slightly more moderate view than that of some contemporary commentators."

But, as she almost always does, the Queen took the criticism onboard, continuing a process of upgrading the running of her household and the quality of her advisors and opening the royal finances to more scrutiny. She volunteered to pay income tax for the first time and backed a cost-cutting regimen that has enabled the budget for her household to remain static for the past two decades. These changes, slow, steady and largely invisible to outsiders, have not only made the monarchy more efficient but in 2010 persuaded Cameron's new coalition government to reform the system of financing the royals, giving the royal household greater autonomy over how the money is spent. "To a large extent, the Queen's life can only work on the basis of doing things that have been done before, but she's very, very receptive to new ideas if they're well argued," says an aide.

Her goal is what Palace insiders term "imperceptible change," modernizing without risking dilution of the royal brand. It's only when one takes the long view that it's clear how far the organization has evolved. The changes in the way it communicates, for example, are stark. The Queen's Christmas message was first televised in 1957. ("That it is possible for some of you to see me today is just another example of the speed at which things are changing all around us," she said.) Since 2006 it has been podcast. After the launch of a royal YouTube channel in 2007, the British Empire version 2.0 has gone on to colonize Facebook, Twitter and Flickr with royal

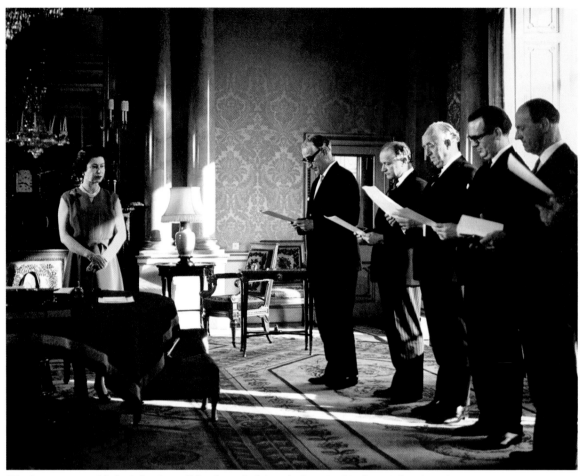

The Queen meets with the Privy Council, her formal advisory body, at Buckingham Palace in 1969

pages and feeds. (More than half a million people "like" the British Monarchy page on Facebook.) These were not decisions slipped past the Queen, but part of a communications strategy developed in close consultation with her.

While she has no concerns about harnessing new technologies, she does have red lines. "There's a real aversion, quite rightly, to anything that's contrived, or a stunt, or is just being done because there happens to be something in the news at that moment that will get an easy headline," says an official.

The Queen has occasionally allowed documentarians to film her but has never much enjoyed the results. *Elizabeth R,* shown in 1992, probably came closest to pleasing both the monarch and the television executives, with its carefully choreographed behind-the-scenes glimpses and some deadpan commentaries by its eponymous heroine. A 2007 TV documentary, *A Year with the Queen,* revealed nothing to surprise or shock, yet triggered contro-

versy after a trailer for it appeared to suggest that the monarch had flounced out of a portrait shoot with the photographer Annie Leibovitz. (The sequences were transposed; the footage recorded her arrival for the sitting, not her departure. And Her Majesty never, ever, flounces.)

The Royal Family, broadcast in 1969, the first TV documentary to portray the Windsors off-duty, drew U.K. audiences of 23 million and a further 350 million worldwide. A fragment released for a Diamond Jubilee exhibition shows why the Queen may well have been right to withhold her permission for it to be broadcast again in its fascinating entirety. The Queen is seen making her family laugh by describing her own battle not to laugh at a formal occasion ("It is extremely difficult sometimes to keep a straight face," she says) and scrambling desperately to make small talk with Richard Nixon, another public figure who would soon learn to regret the recording of private conversations. Decades later,

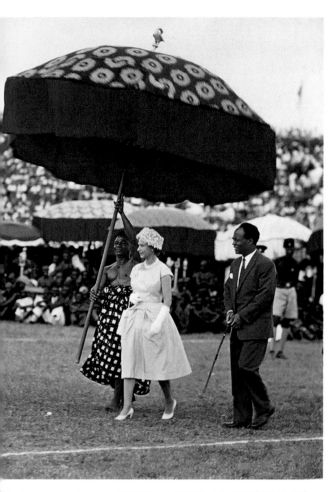

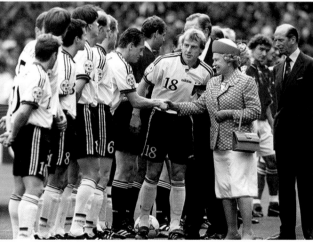

A visit to Commonwealth member Ghana, 1960;
meeting the German soccer team in London, 1996

the Queen's daughter, Princess Anne, dismissed the 1969 documentary as "a rotten idea. The attention that had been brought on one ever since one was a child, you just didn't want any more. The last thing you needed was greater access."

A Future in England's Dreaming

The Queen can be flinty, even intimidating, though diva-like histrionics have never been part of her repertoire. "She is ultimately a practical and levelheaded person. You know the standards that you've got to achieve, and you know you've got to achieve them all the time with her," says an official. In his recent biography *Diamond Queen,* Andrew Marr described what typically happens to those who disappoint. "She never argues, she just looks at the person very blankly," a source told Marr. "The corners of her mouth don't turn down. It's not a hostile look. It's just a complete blank—and it's devastating." It should be no surprise that a woman who has spent six decades perfecting the art of putting members of the public at ease has also acquired a parallel ability to discomfit.

Talking to the Queen, properly talking to her rather than exchanging banal pleasantries as she performs one of her regular visits to schools, hospitals, businesses, military units or charities, quickly reveals her to be sharp of mind—and tongue. She is interested in politics but not obviously partisan. She has held weekly audiences with every Prime Minister from Winston Churchill on. Neither monarch nor ministers reveal the precise topics discussed, but many premiers—and there have been 12 during her reign—have spoken of her wisdom. "What I found to be her most surprising attribute is how streetwise she is," Tony Blair told another biographer, Robert Hardman. "Frequently throughout my time as Prime Minister, I was always stunned by her total ability to pick up the public mood and define it in the conversations I had with her." David Cameron cites "her huge knowledge of other countries. She has traveled incredibly widely, and that shines through in conversation with her. Whether it's Saudi Arabia, Canada or Tuvalu, she's been there and knows the issues."

She can be unexpectedly forthright, and her sense of humor runs from the sly to the slapstick. Describing the conferring of a knighthood on a well-known entertainer, the Queen points at the burnt-orange rug on which she and her guests are standing to indicate the once pale-skinned performer's improbable shade of tan. She can also laugh at herself. Prince Andrew, rumored to be her favorite child, tells of a family dinner at which he distracted the Queen with a question just as she stood up to leave the table. A footman pulled away her chair "very properly," says

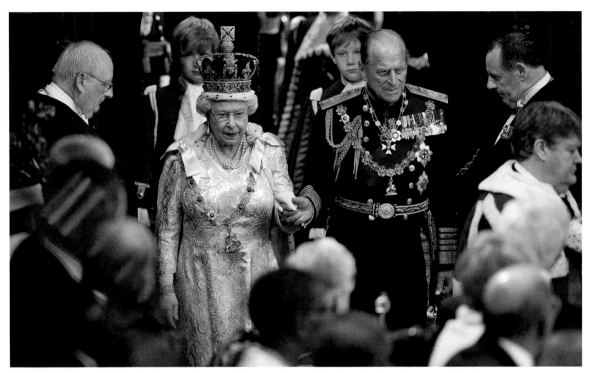

Escorted by Prince Philip, the Queen arrives to address the House of Lords at the State Opening of Parliament, 2010

her son. "She sat down again, except there was no chair. Everyone, including the Queen, laughed and laughed—and of course she reassured the terrified footman he had done nothing wrong."

There's a tendency to assume the royals are more fragile and pampered than ordinary folk. In fact, they often turn out to be unusually robust. Palace life can be surprisingly austere, and family members are further toughened by boarding schools and the males by military training and in some cases deployments. It is also true that the microculture of palace life breeds a distinct and separate species. Chatting with TIME in 2006, Prince Andrew mused on his upbringing: "People say to me, 'Would you like to swap your life with me for 24 hours? Your life must be very strange.' But of course I have not experienced any other life. It's not strange to me. [It's] the same way with the Queen. She has never experienced anything else."

That is not strictly true. Born in 1926 to the second son of King George V, "Lilibet" was able to enjoy a life of quiet privilege until the death of her grandfather and the unexpected abdication of his heir, her uncle, King Edward VIII, who chose Wallis Simpson over destiny and duty. His decision shaped Princess Elizabeth's destiny—and her attitude to duty.

From the moment of her father's accession in 1936, she prepared for her own accession. She has cultivated no known vices, works long hours, appears more indulgent to her beloved dogs than to her children and more indulgent to them than to herself. Choosing Philip, a comparatively impoverished scion of the ousted Greek monarchy, as her husband is probably the closest she has ever come to putting her own interests first, yet even that decision turned out well. Prince Philip may not be a natural diplomat, but his pithy and politically incorrect pronouncements have added to the gaiety of nations, or at least of his adopted nation, and he has sublimated his own ambitions to supporting his wife. Prince Harry told Marr, "Regardless of whether my grandfather seems to be doing his own thing, sort of wandering off like a fish down a river, the fact that he's there—personally, I don't think she could do it without him, especially when they're both at this age."

The Queen has a close relationship with her grandchildren, especially William and Harry, in some respects closer than with her own children. She may have mellowed or—perish the thought—learned from Diana to be more emotionally available; she certainly made efforts to comfort and compensate her bereaved grandsons for their loss. As a young mother, she was no Diana. Her determination to serve her country meant her children put up with long absences. In 1953, the new Queen and her husband left their toddlers, Charles and Anne, for a protracted state tour. Andrew and Edward, born after their mother's coronation, never knew a time when their father did not trail two steps behind their mother in public, as protocol dictates. If they sometimes find themselves straddling a gap between their realities and the wider world's, that's hardly surprising.

As a result, none of the Queen's offspring have enjoyed an untroubled relationship with that wider world. They can seem arrogant. They can appear spendthrift. Anne at least carved out a career as an equestrian. The younger sons lack direction. The oldest, Charles, has direction but no momentum. The Queen's extraordinary staying power has con-

signed her heir to a long apprenticeship.

Her popularity has barely flickered during crises, but she will not be around to witness the greatest challenge the monarchy faces—to manage without her. "She's so dedicated and really determined to finish everything she started," Prince William told Robert Hardman. "She'll want to hand over knowing she's done everything she possibly could to help, and that she's got no regrets and no unfinished business; that she's done everything she can for the country and that she's not let anyone down—she minds an awful lot about that." The final test of Monarchy Inc.'s savvy CEO will be whether the organization remains as strong—and as unexpectedly relevant—over the next 60 years as the one she will leave behind.

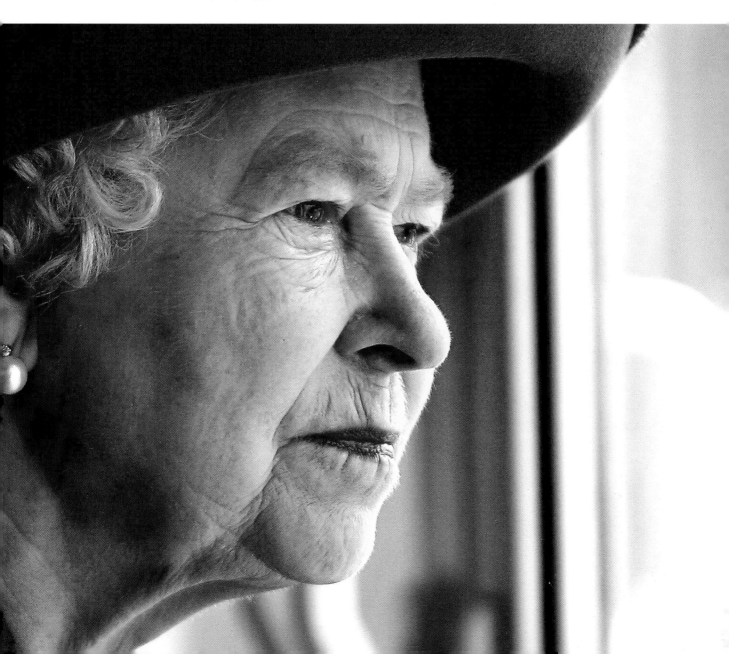

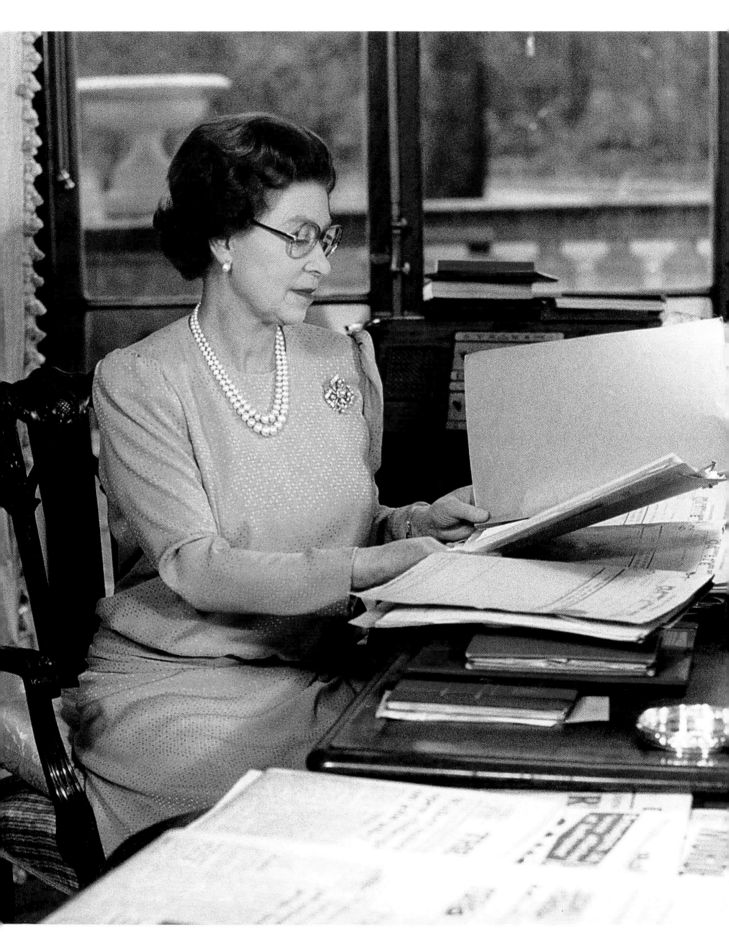

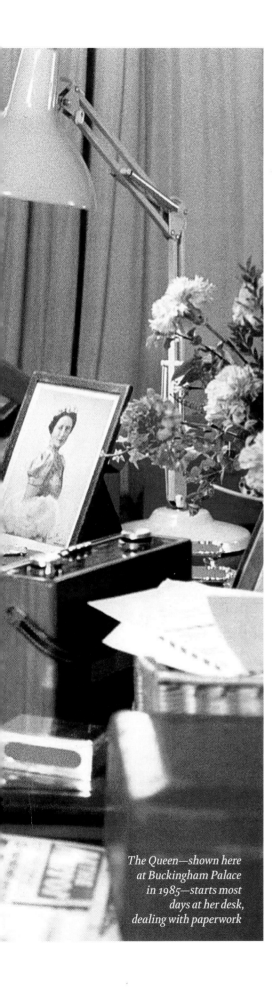

The Queen—shown here at Buckingham Palace in 1985—starts most days at her desk, dealing with paperwork

How They Earn Their Keep

The Queen and her family are always working, but it's not always obvious just what they do

By Catherine Mayer

T he 19th-century North London church of St. Michael's was once a proud institution, the center of the community. By the late-20th century, like Britain's monarchy, it risked falling into disrepair and irrelevance. If its history—and its resurgence in recent years—struck a chord of recognition with the Prince of Wales, he didn't let it show during his February 2012 visit. Whether admiring the nave's soaring arches or chatting to the school pupils and representatives of voluntary organizations assembled beneath them, the heir to the throne maintained an expression of amiable interest. "What's so lovely is that he's easy and comfortable with so many different groups of people," enthused the parish rector, Rev. Philip North, as his royal guest pressed a final hand, mouthed a few more words of appreciation and slid onto the leather seat of his limousine. "You could introduce him to a 7-year-old child and a man with mental health problems and a Muslim woman, and he handled every situation completely beautifully. Everyone had a sense of being treated specially."

Rev. North has expanded on the work of the previous rector

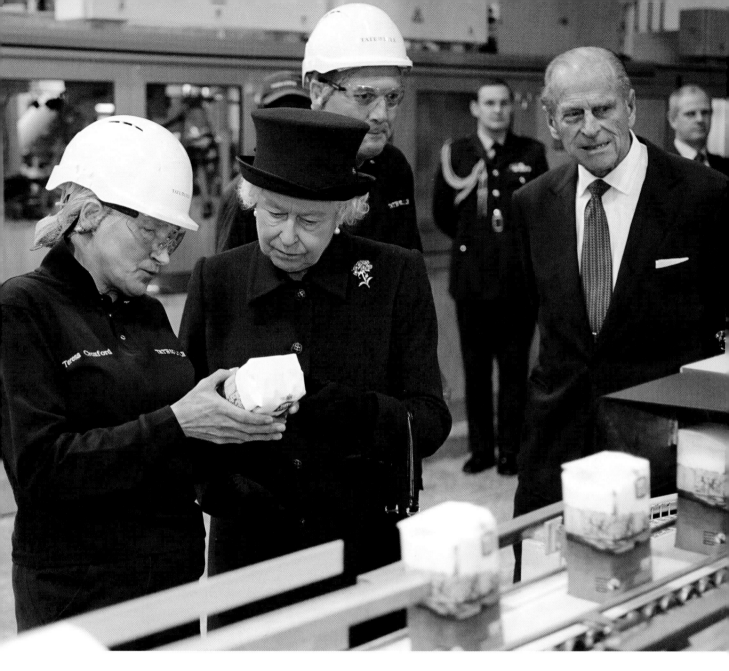

of St. Michael's to rescue the structure and rebuild the congregation from a low point a decade and a half earlier. When and if Prince Charles accedes to the throne, he will aim to keep up the Queen's strategies to strengthen the monarchy after a nadir that coincided with St. Michael's. The Prince carries some responsibility for that nadir. The Queen has gone about being royal steadily and impressively. Her children have found the job harder to master.

Her oldest is no slacker at the workaday aspects of his role and can do small talk with the best of them. But the 1992 breakdowns of his marriage and his brother Andrew's drew attention to what royals might be up to when they weren't visiting churches, planting trees or assuring factory workers that they found the widgets they produced re-

ally jolly interesting. It wasn't just the revelation that the Windsors and their spouses could behave as badly as ordinary folk; it was the thought of them doing so onboard the royal train or just off the polo field or atop sun-loungers in the South of France— at the expense of those factory workers and other taxpayers. As the Princes called time on their failed relationships, Britons examined their own relationships with the monarchy, revisiting the perennial question of whether the royals—and what the royals contribute to public life—represented good value for their state funding, just as it hit a new peak of $139.7 million.

There was one simple way to appease public opinion: cut spending and find efficiency savings. By 2011 the bill for Britain's head of state had been

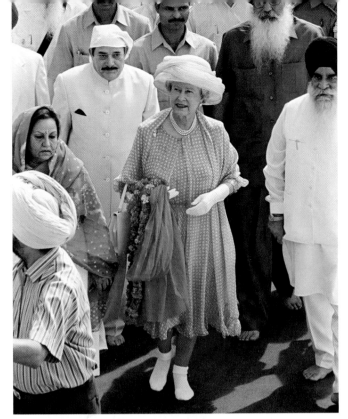

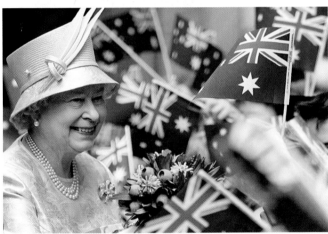

Clockwise from left: The Queen and Prince Philip inspect the production line at a London sugar refinery in 2008; the Queen at a temple in the Punjab, India, in 1997, and at the opening of the Commonwealth Games in Sydney, 2006

Prince Charles converse earnestly with the volunteers and staff of C4WS, an initiative that invites the homeless to sleep in St. Michael's and other churches during the coldest months of the year, it's easy to see the immediate fillip to morale this interaction delivers and to anticipate the profile boost it may yield to such an excellent charity. But there have been no scientific cost-benefit analyses of the value of such public duties or of the royals' value to British tourism, much less of the monarchy's most tenuous contribution of all—to the value of Britain's national identity and stability. No wonder there are grumbles when the Windsors appear to be living high on the hog or down in the mud. No wonder the more minor Windsors occasionally seek to allay existential doubts by trying to hold down proper jobs.

They have done so with notably mixed success. The royal role can be a full-time occupation, and a surprisingly meaningful one, as a closer look at the Queen's routines bears out. But being a royal and someone else's employee can be royally problematic, as several of her family members have discovered.

A Woman's Work

The Queen's mornings begin with a modest breakfast and, if she's in residence at Buckingham Palace, Windsor Castle, Holyroodhouse or Balmoral, the wheeze of bagpipes at 9 a.m. By the time the daily 15-minute serenade is done, she is making serious inroads into paperwork she started the night before. There is no constitutional need for her to do so, but she is determined to keep abreast of the news, especially from her kingdom, realms, the wider Commonwealth and her military forces. She reads and answers private correspondence and burrows through a mound of documents sent by her government and her ambassadors. She sees the minutes from every Cabinet meeting and initials them to signify she has had sight of them. Her signature is required for parliamentary bills to pass into law and for diplomatic postings to be filled.

Like the bagpipe serenade—her pleasure in which, as she recently confessed to a guest at a state dinner, has paled after 60 years—these conventions continue partly because to end them would be to raise uncomfortable questions about other areas of redundancy in the institution of monarchy. Nobody knows exactly what would happen if the Queen sud-

slashed to $51.4 million. The Queen now receives $12.6 million to cover the expenses of her household. The rest goes for travel, the maintenance of the royal palaces and other expenses. She faces a pay cut of about 14% in 2013 in return for more autonomy over her finances.

The new system is designed to be more transparent than the funding mechanisms it replaces but still won't reflect the total price tag of the monarchy for Britons. There are hidden costs to royal occasions, not least the expense of policing them. The benefits can be equally hard to assess. Watching

denly refused to deploy her pen. She never blocks bills or objects to candidates. She is called "defender of the faith," but never meddles in church affairs. She is the head of Britain's armed forces, but has no powers to deploy them. She is the "fount of justice," but doesn't administer the law.

Many royal protocols and procedures are based around traditions that evolved when the monarch wielded power as well as influence. That means much of what the sovereign does these days is theater. At the State Opening of Parliament, the ceremony to mark the beginning of each new legislative session, she outlines the government's plans, but she has no direct input into them. Though the details of her weekly meetings with the Prime Minister of the day remain private, it's unlikely that Her Majesty ventures into the detail of policy.

To assume the royal theater is without impact is to underestimate the force of imagery and the Queen's global pull. In many respects her role differs little from that of many ceremonial heads of state, elected or hereditary: heavy on symbolism, light on executive action. Where it is unique is in its scope and volume. Nobody else serves as head of state for so many countries. Few other heads of state can rival her fame, and it's hard to think of any head of state—at any rate, a benign one—who is so inextricably bound up in his or her nation's self-image.

As a result, a big chunk of the Queen's time is taken up by people who simply want to meet her. Her diary contains as many as 430 of these smaller engagements every year. She holds audiences most mornings with diplomats, bishops, judges and members of the military. Sometimes she presides at investitures—hour-long ceremonies at which she presents decorations, medals and orders to as many as 100 honorees, with an aide standing nearby to murmur their names and biographical details as they approach. Her afternoons often involve visits to schools, businesses and the institutions that make up part of British life. She cuts ribbons, unveils plaques, and christens ships. At every event, she exchanges pleasantries with as many attendees as can be arranged into what one aide calls "orderly horseshoes" (a configuration that allows each person to hear the monarch as she moves from one interlocutor to the next). She and Prince Philip regularly host small lunches, surprisingly informal events at which Campari and

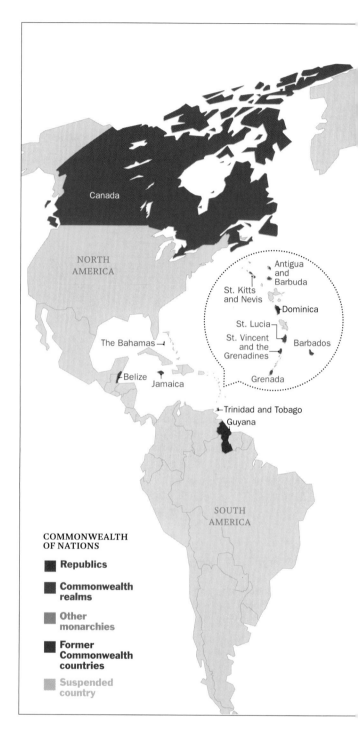

fine wines flow freely, the Queen's dogs recline under the dining table, and the only factor linking guests from disparate fields is their surprise to have received the gold-edged invitation.

There are bigger, set-piece events, too: There are garden parties in the palace grounds that blend several flavors of Britishness—summer rain, anemic sandwiches and hats that often seem more animate than

Commonwealth of Nations

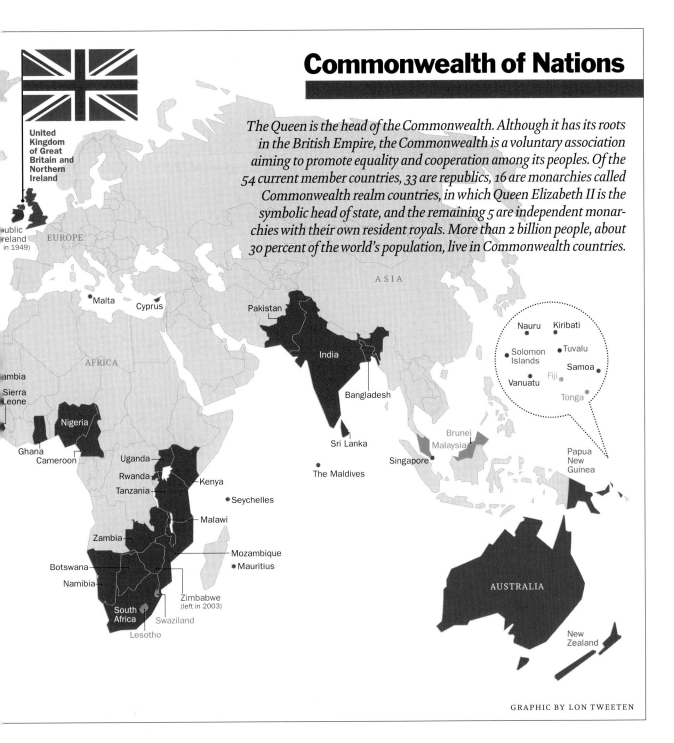

The Queen is the head of the Commonwealth. Although it has its roots in the British Empire, the Commonwealth is a voluntary association aiming to promote equality and cooperation among its peoples. Of the 54 current member countries, 33 are republics, 16 are monarchies called Commonwealth realm countries, in which Queen Elizabeth II is the symbolic head of state, and the remaining 5 are independent monarchies with their own resident royals. More than 2 billion people, about 30 percent of the world's population, live in Commonwealth countries.

United Kingdom of Great Britain and Northern Ireland

ublic reland in 1949)

EUROPE

ASIA

Malta

Cyprus

Pakistan

India

Nauru   Kiribati

Solomon Islands   Tuvalu

Samoa

Vanuatu   Fiji

Tonga

AFRICA

ambia

Sierra Leone

Nigeria

Ghana

Cameroon

Uganda

Rwanda

Tanzania

Kenya

Seychelles

Malawi

Zambia

Mozambique

Mauritius

Botswana

Namibia

Zimbabwe (left in 2003)

South Africa

Swaziland

Lesotho

Bangladesh

Sri Lanka

The Maldives

Singapore

Brunei

Malaysia

Papua New Guinea

AUSTRALIA

New Zealand

their owners; evening receptions that bring together leaders from particular fields of endeavor or mix and match cross-sections of society. And twice a year, once in the spring and once in the fall, there are state visits. The government asks the Queen to invite foreign heads of state to stay, and she never disappoints, however much she may wish to do so. She reportedly found the 1978 state visit of Romanian dictator Nico-

lae Ceausescu and his wife, Elena, so distasteful that she avoided them whenever possible during their sojourn at Buckingham Palace, darting behind a bush when she spotted them heading toward her in the gardens. Most state visits prove more convivial. The 101st such visit hosted by the Queen, in May 2011, saw her extend a warm welcome to the Obamas. It may not have changed the substance of U.S.-British

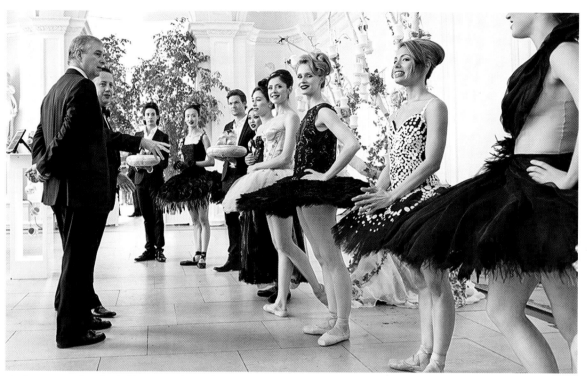

Andrew is introduced to ballerinas at the English National Ballet's summer 2011 party in London

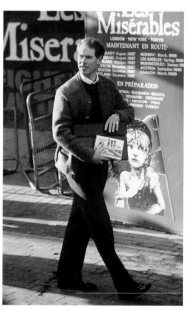

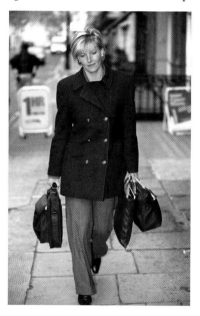

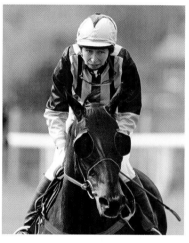

From left: Edward going to work at the Palace Theatre, 1988; his future wife, Sophie Rhys-Jones, heading to the office, 1998; Anne riding for charity, 1992

relations, but film and photographs of the President and his wife enjoying the Queen's hospitality helped allay fears that he harbored a secret grudge against the British for the torture of his grandfather in a Kenyan prison during that country's struggle against British colonial rule.

The British monarchy has an active outreach program too. The Queen's 2011 visit to the Republic of Ireland, the first by a U.K. sovereign since Ireland's 1919–21 war of independence, marked a moment of reconciliation between the once fractious neighbors. The experience was "electrifying," says a Palace official who traveled with the royal party. "You get used to seeing what half a million people look like, if you're doing a visit to Africa and you're going from Kampala to Entebbe and you've got everyone lined in the streets, and they're all cheering, and that's very good. But the strange thing about Ireland was

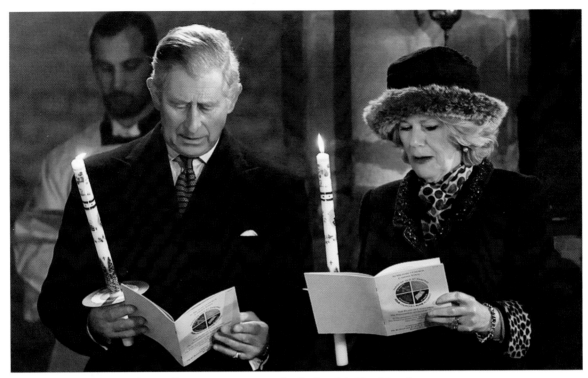

Charles and Camilla attend a Candlemas service at St. Michael's church in North London, 2012

the first day of almost standing there in silence. Not threatening, but sort of respectful silence, almost saying, 'Well, let's see what you're going to give us.' And by the final day, they were cheering."

The Queen's children and, more recently, her grandsons William and Harry carry out official trips too. To celebrate the Diamond Jubilee, royals are being dispatched to every realm and a number of Commonwealth countries, Crown dependencies and British overseas territories. William and Kate's schedule includes Malaysia, Singapore, the Solomon Islands and Tuvalu, while Harry drew the cushier combination of Belize, Jamaica and the Bahamas.

Kate is a newcomer to the business but won rave reviews for her first official trip as a royal, to Canada and the U.S. in summer 2011. Her husband and his brother learned the ropes watching their parents work the rope lines—Diana was a mistress of the walkabout, accepting flowers and sticky kisses from toddlers and always seeming to know just where the cameras were.

That's not as easy as it looks, but if the daily grind of royal life—the glad-handing and the chitchat and the need to evince interest in tedious things—is hard work, the bigger problem for the royals is what to do with themselves the rest of the time. And here, too,

the older generation has provided useful object lessons, if not always positive examples.

Heirs and Disgraces

Despite a divorce and the odd tangle with the press, for whom she can never quite conceal her visceral loathing, Princess Anne has navigated the pressures of combining a public role with a private career better than her siblings. She has been a distinguished horsewoman, winning trophies and representing Britain in the 1976 Olympics. She encouraged her daughter, Zara Phillips, to follow her into the equestrian arena but spared both her children the pressures of representing the monarchy by turning down titles for them.

Military service is the closest most Windsor men get to experiencing normalcy. All the male Windsors apart from Princess Anne's son, Peter Phillips, and the Queen's youngest, Edward, have served Queen and country in the military. The Prince of Wales briefly commanded a minehunter, though he was never deployed to a conflict. Andrew also rose through naval ranks to take charge of a minehunter after serving as a helicopter pilot aboard the carrier HMS *Invincible* as part of the British task force dispatched to retake the Falkland Islands when Ar-

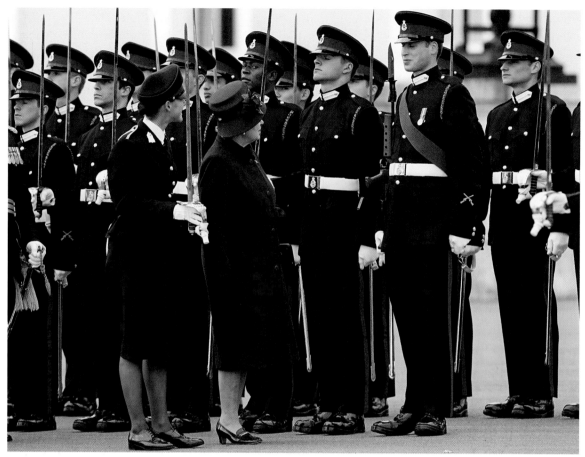

The Queen inspects officers graduating from the military academy Sandhurst in 2006, including William (second from right)

gentinian troops invaded. His nephew William's six-week deployment to the Falklands in 2012, on what the U.K. government insisted was a routine tour of duty as a search-and-rescue helicopter pilot, coincided with the 30th anniversary of the conflict over the archipelago Argentina calls the "Malvinas" and regards as its own sovereign territory. Its foreign ministry issued a terse statement: "The Argentine people regret that the royal heir will arrive on [our] national soil in the uniform of the conqueror and not with the wisdom of the statesman who works in the service of peace and dialogue among nations."

If William's presence in the Falklands could be interpreted as provocative, Prince Harry's 2007 deployment to Afghanistan, where he coordinated air support for military operations on the ground, threatened to blow a royal raspberry not only at the enemy the Prince dubbed "Terry Taliban" but also at any al Qaeda-inspired groups operating in the area, potentially endangering the troops serving alongside the royal target. "There's no way I'm going to put my-self through [the royal military academy] Sandhurst and then sit on my arse back home while my boys are out fighting for their country," Harry had said in a 2006 interview. "I do enjoy running down a ditch full of mud, firing bullets. It's the way I am. I love it."

A news blackout agreed to by British media enabled the Prince to satisfy his yen for action for two months before recalcitrant foreign outlets revealed his whereabouts. He's widely expected to deploy back to Afghanistan during 2012. As a Palace source points out, Harry's training to fly Apache helicopters was far from cheap; not to exploit his expensively acquired skills would be to squander that money.

If such royal deployments aren't free from risk or controversy, they are a walk in the park compared to the sniper's alley run by Windsors who enter the commercial world. Prince Edward opted for a career in television, founding the independent program maker Ardent Productions. It lurched from one misadventure to another, drawing the wrath of Edward's own family in September 2001, when an Ardent crew was spotted filming at St. Andrews University, in breach of guidelines agreed to by the media to allow undergraduate Prince William to study in privacy.

Edward's wife, Sophie, had suffered a spot of bother over conflict of interest earlier in the same year, when transcripts were published of a conversation covertly taped by British Sunday tabloid *News of the World* (later shuttered in the wake of a phone-hacking scandal). The Countess of Wessex believed she was speaking to a potential client for her public relations business, a wealthy Middle Easterner. "In your own country, when people find we're working for you, the chances are you'll get people interested: 'Oh gosh, they've employed the Countess of Wessex's PR company,'" she said. Unfortunately for Sophie, she was talking to Mazher Mahmood, an undercover reporter. She severed ties with the company she had founded, in mute acknowledgment that her career in reputational enhancement presaged reputational damage for the monarchy. In 2010 Mahmood repeated the ruse, coaxing Sarah, Duchess of York, into promising him access to her ex-husband, Prince Andrew, for $800,000.

The incident provided a different angle on the value of the royal family. "Fergie" believed entrée to her husband to be worth more than three-quarters of a million dollars. Britain's tabloid press more often depicts Andrew as worthless, a "playboy prince" so profligate in his use of subsidized travel that they taunt him as "Air Miles Andy." The truth lies somewhere in between. Since the end of his naval career, Andrew has struggled to find a gainful occupation. As the U.K.'s special representative for trade and investment, he did rack up air miles—promoting British companies and interests. In 2011 he relinquished his formal government role amid criticism of his conduct. He had chosen friends unwisely—not least the U.S. financier Jeffrey Epstein, with whom the Pirnce was photographed taking a stroll in New York City's Central Park two years after Epstein's conviction for soliciting prostitution. Andrew had also cultivated contacts in the Middle East and North Africa, including Saif Gaddafi. Palace sources insist he did so at the behest of the British government, the same reason his mother invited the Ceausescus to stay

Everybody wants to meet the royals—and the royals meet everybody, from vicars, community workers and U.S. presidents to tabloid reporters, sex offenders and dictators. It may not be a job in the conventional sense. But it's what being royal is all about.

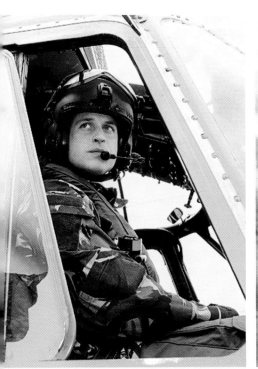 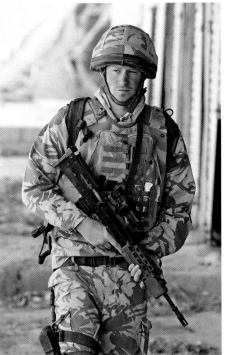 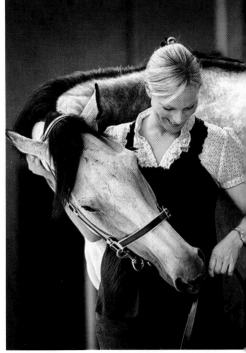

William flies a helicopter during an exercise, 2011; Harry patrols in Afghanistan, 2008; and cousin Zara at the stables, 2009

The Man Who Will Be King

He was born to rule, but it was left to Prince Charles to figure out what to do in the meantime

By Belinda Luscombe

If the British monarchy is a peculiar institution, as enormously influential as it is essentially powerless, then Prince Charles occupies the weirdest place within it. He's the next king, the future of one of the foundational establishments of British society, the heir to 400 years' worth of history. Yet much of the country seems to treat him like a dolt.

Everybody loves Queen Elizabeth. Her longevity and pint-sized, no-nonsense robustness are as British as hedgerows. Everybody loves the Duke and Duchess of Cambridge, Will and Kate. Their cheery elegance and glamour are as British as a rose garden.

Then there's Charles, as British as a boggy field.

The future sovereign of the United Kingdom may have the signature honor of being the most widely mocked heir to any throne ever. He has been lampooned for saying he wanted to live inside the trousers of his current wife, Camilla. He has been ridiculed for his utterances on the environment—"I just come and talk to the plants, really, very important to

talk to them. They respond, I find." And comedian and puppet alike have parodied his voice and face.

The country is split on whether he *should* be the next king. According to the most recent polls, around 46% of Britons would like the 63-year-old Charles to pass the crown directly to William, without popping it on his own head first. That isn't going to happen. Being king is not a job you earn; it is a job you inherit. Being worthy of it is optional. And in fact Charles is worthy, even though he has taken an unlikely route to get there.

Not very tall or good-looking or especially athletic, Charles Philip Arthur George is a tricky individual on whom to pin a fantasy like royal lineage. Young women of the 1970s did not swoon in droves over marrying him when he was single, as their present-day counterparts did until recently over William and still do over Harry. He has a strange voice, an odd demeanor and, while genuine and earnest, does not radiate warmth the way his sons do. One British writer called him a "one-man awkward squad." When he finally did get married, in 1981, the wedding had all

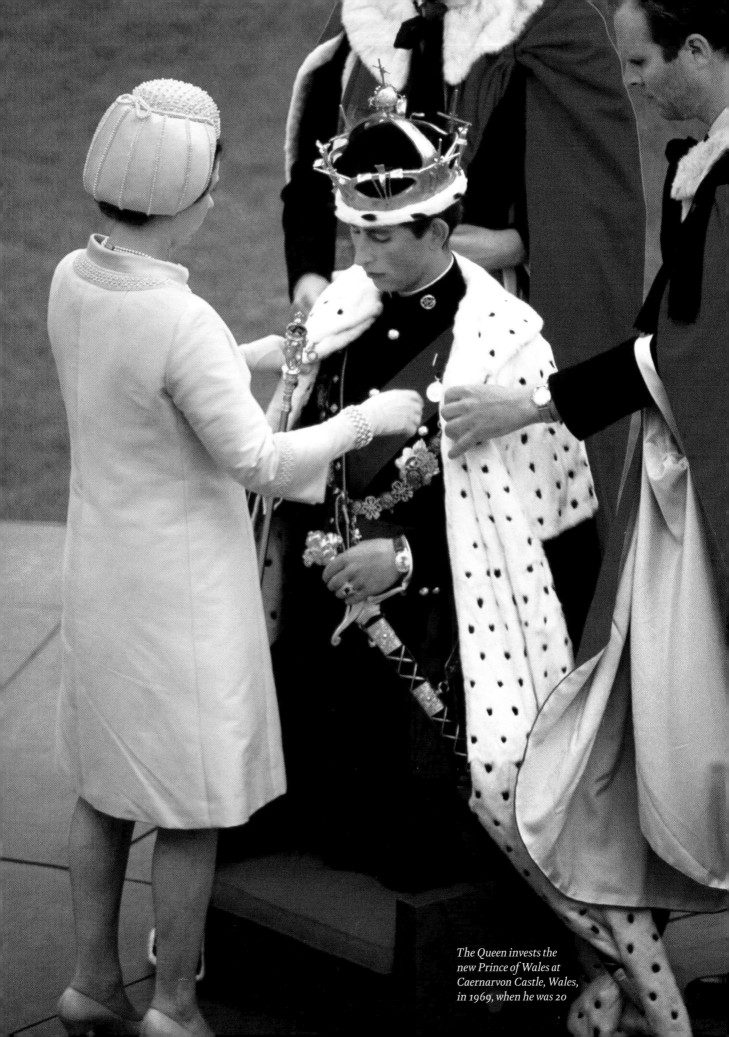

The Queen invests the new Prince of Wales at Caernarvon Castle, Wales, in 1969, when he was 20

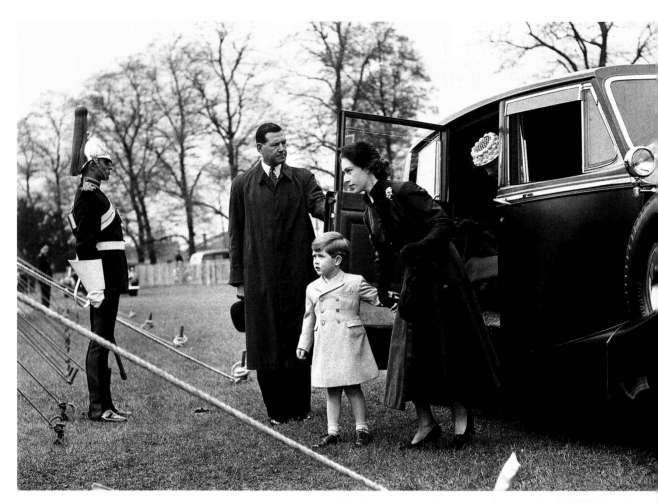

the ceremony and glamour the age could muster, but the marriage proved to be a total bust. Charles and Diana stuck it out barely a decade before the Prime Minister announced they were separating.

At the time, it seemed that Charles had horribly mismanaged his one real responsibility—to get married and then produce and raise a couple of majestikins—and worse, it was all because he couldn't stay faithful to his wife. The royal family is, after all, a family. If the future king can't even get that part right, what on earth is he doing in the job?

Charles was brought up to preside over two institutions that changed under him: royalty and family. When his mother came to the throne at the age of 25, he was 3 years old. Britain was still emerging from the privations and losses of the war. The burden of lifting the British people's sprits had fallen heavily on the royal family; it was believed the stress of it contributed to Charles' grandfather's death at 57.

The qualities a future sovereign would need were clear: mental toughness, steadfastness and doughty

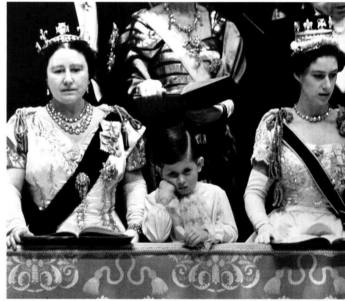

Clockwise from top left: Princess Margaret and her nephew arrive at a horse show, 1953; mother and son, 1969; one year earlier, at his installation as a knight in the Most Noble Order of the Garter; Charles, 4, with his grandmother and aunt at his mother's coronation in 1953

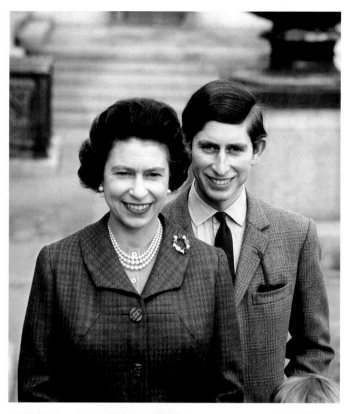

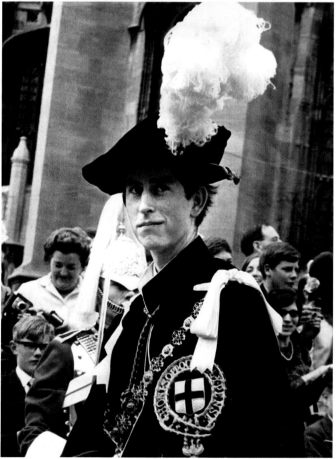

cheer in the face of adversity. Adroitness, a sense of the public hive mind and an ability to harness current trends were suspect traits, more suited for movie stars and marketeers. And marrying for love was for kings who abdicated.

Thus Charles was sent to Gordonstoun, a Scottish boarding school known for its ability to stiffen an upper lip. When not there, he was at Buckingham Palace—a home with many assets, but not exactly cozy or welcoming—or holidaying in the austere grandeur of Balmoral in Scotland. It was a childhood calculated to foster a sense of separation.

But what the public expected from royalty was shifting. The Queen cautiously opened a tiny gap in the heavy drapes that shielded the family from view. She expanded the "walkabout," the time a monarch spends personally greeting people. She addressed her subjects on TV. She opened the state rooms of the palace to the public.

They were small but politically shrewd and necessary moves. She could not know that once the genie of public access was uncorked, he would never return to the bottle. Gradually, as the public's interest in royalty became an appetite and then a craving, technology and the expanding media conspired to jimmy the life of their royal highnesses wide open. Charles found himself starring in a global reality show over which he had little control and in which he seemed ill-suited to participate.

The biography of Prince Charles on the official website of the British monarchy is 17 paragraphs long. Two paragraphs deal with his lineage and right to the throne. Nine paragraphs deal with Diana. Perhaps this is not disproportionate; Diana's arrival, departure and subsequent death changed everything.

Their marriage went about as badly as marriages can go, with infidelity, work-life imbalance and poor conflict resolution. And it went cockeyed in public. The royal reality show had a very special episode in which the future king's wife went on television to tell viewers that His Royal Highness couldn't keep it in his pants and to name the other woman, who was also married: Camilla Parker Bowles.

After Charles and Diana separated in 1992, his popularity went into stomach-churning freefall. In 1991, 82% of Britons thought he would make a good king. By 1996, that number was 41%. In 1984, during his marriage to Diana, half the respondents to a poll

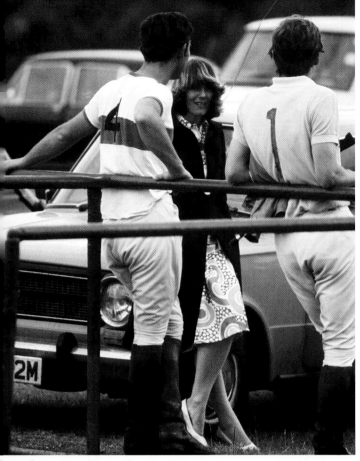

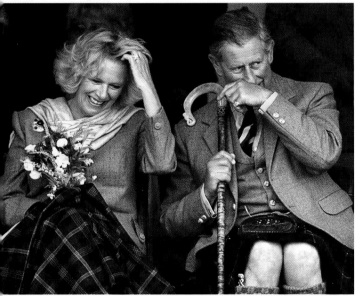

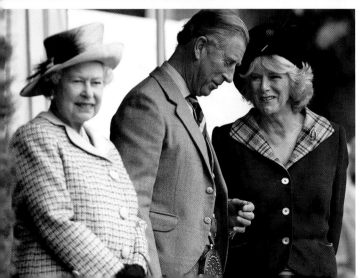

nominated him as one of their two or three favorite royals. In 1994, only 16% did.

With his marriage, Charles found himself yet again part of an institution that had profoundly changed in the time he had spent preparing for it. He was not the only one caught out; he and Diana separated just a year before divorce hit its peak level in Britain. The marital shift had been long coming, brought about by changes in the status of women, access to family planning, and the general loosening of divorce law. Even more fundamental was the transformation of marriage from an obligatory institution whose purpose was mostly to raise children to a more or less temporary agreement between two people to make each other deliriously happy.

But Charles—and his brother Andrew, who also divorced in 1996—had been brought up in such a bubble that they had not fully grasped how seismic the changes were. (Charles' godfather and chief mentor, Lord Mountbatten, had even advised him to choose a young and inexperienced woman.) As with most of life in the royal family, being a spouse was a duty. Nobody, least of all women lucky enough to be brought under the bejeweled wing of the Palace, was supposed to regard it as enjoyable or even optional.

If royalty is an accident of birth, then popularity was an accident of Charles' marriage. So when he threw it over, it was almost as if he had used the royal anointing spoon to stir his coffee or, Esau-like, had traded his birthright for a mess of pottage (although Camilla was called much crueler things at the time). In many ways, Charles' post-Diana life can be seen as a dogged burrowing back into public approval. Having lost the respect he had never actually earned, he had to win it back by working for it.

First, he set his personal life in order. Charles and Camilla started quietly living together in 2003 and married in a subdued but soigné affair in 2005. While at first she drew unflattering comparisons to Diana—how could he have cast off the doe-eyed beauty for that old boot?—gradually her warmth and jolliness grew on people. And because she had been in Charles' circle before his marriage, many

From top: Charles and Camilla, in their 20s, at a polo match, c. 1975; still enjoying each other three decades later, at the Mey Highland Games in Scotland, 2005, and at the Braemar Highland Games the following year

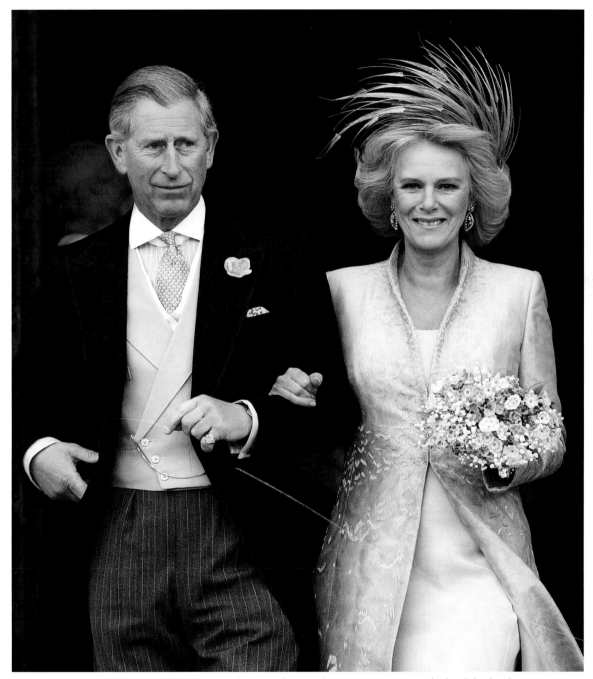

Prince Charles and the new Dutchess of Cornwall were wed on April 9, 2005, in a ceremony both subdued and soigné

people could reconfigure the story as that of a couple who never got over their first love.

Princes William and Harry are reported to have developed an affection for Camilla, and she has, like Charles, done the hard yards at ribbon-cuttings and old people's homes. Plus, unlike Diana, she's discreet; if she's fazed by what people say about her, she doesn't let it show. In a sign of a shift in the prevailing opinion of her, there has been some grudging admission that she's actually rather good-looking, in the right light. By the time the two got married, almost two-thirds of Brits said they were fine with it.

Charles, meanwhile, set about pursuing some of his other less tabloid-worthy passions, particularly around the environment. He was an early and usually well-informed advocate of sustainability. And this time the ground tilted in his favor; many of the seemingly unorthodox ideas he championed have

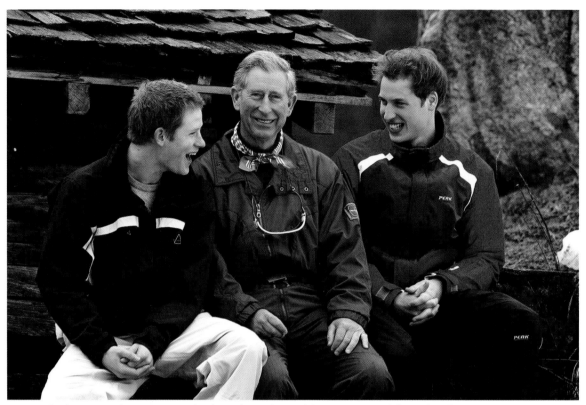

Prince Charles seems to have maintained a close relationship with his sons, Harry (left), and William

come to be accepted as mainstream. In 2007 Charles committed to having his household, Clarence House, lower its carbon footprint by 50% in five years. The Prince's Audi, Jaguar and Range Rover were duly re-engineered to run on used cooking oil. The royal train, one of the Prince's favored modes of transport for middle distances, was also converted. Wood-chip boilers and reed-bed sewage systems were installed at his stately homes wherever possible. And his newest residence, Llwynywermod, is protected against the damp Welsh air partly with natural sheep's-wool insulation.

Yes, these are the esoteric activities of a person with too much money and time at his disposal. But who better than a prince—a man whose main job is to consider the long-range future of his country—to pioneer the development of such innovations? Who else besides a wildly wealthy public servant to do the R&D for worthy causes nobody else can pursue?

In a similar way, the Prince's line of foodstuffs, Duchy Originals, is trying to find a way to bring food to market using what are considered more sustainable but less market-friendly production techniques. (Charles has long been opposed to genetically modi-

fied foods.) There have been some kinks in the line; in 2011 the brand had $3.5 million in profits, but only gave $985,000 to charity because of shortfalls from previous years that had to be made up.

And then there's the Prince's Trust, which has the kind of do-goodery mission of "helping change young lives" that might seem too broad to actually do any good, but which is, by many reports, well run and effective. Enough so, that although even the 1% think of him as the 1%, when the Prince gave a speech in working-class Tottenham after the London riots of August 2011, he was met warmly.

Not all His Royal Highness's efforts to effect public change have been so welcome. He's considered to be a bit of a namby-pamby sentimentalist when it comes to architecture. He recently put the kibosh on a development by Lord Richard Rogers, one of Britain's most revered modern architects, by writing to a friend in the Qatari royal family, one of the funders.

His handwritten letters to members of Parliament—called "black spider memos" for their busy underlines and exclamation points—protesting or suggesting changes to the way the government is going about its business are greeted by turns with alarm and humor. Some of them pertain to changes in the way the royals are paid. Others have to do with his causes. While the contents are rarely revealed, the recipients never doubt their future sovereign's passion. By convention, the royal family is not allowed to so much as nibble at the edge of politics. The Prince is allowed, however, to offer elected officials advice on matters of state.

Again, worthy efforts such as these only serve to make Charles seem like a man trying to find a way to be useful when he has considerable resources and influence but no real job. They keep him from being idle as he fiddles around in destiny's waiting room.

One side-effect of waiting so long to ascend the throne has been materially beneficial, however. The Prince has been able to spend more time being a father. Indeed, he has had to. And perhaps because his own childhood was not so ideal, he has worked pretty hard at it. Even when his popularity was at its lowest, polls still showed that three-quarters of his people approved of the job he was doing with his offspring.

Charles took care that the press, which intruded so much on his life, was kept out of his sons'. They have been allowed to form friendships and make mistakes largely out of the public eye. William and Kate's marriage was much more sensibly managed than his and Diana's. The couple had plenty of time to get to know each other, and William appears to have been allowed to choose his bride almost as freely as any other 28-year-old.

Concern for his family is one very good reason Charles will not pass the crown directly to his vastly more popular son. He saw the toll it took on his mother and on his siblings when she was consumed with public duties at such a young age. And he realized it's not good for the future of the monarchy.

Charles has worked hard to earn back the respect of his people. But he will be king whether the people want him or not. The primary role of the royal family is to survive and regenerate. If Charles' greatest achievement is to ensure his son is better loved than he is, he will have done his duty.

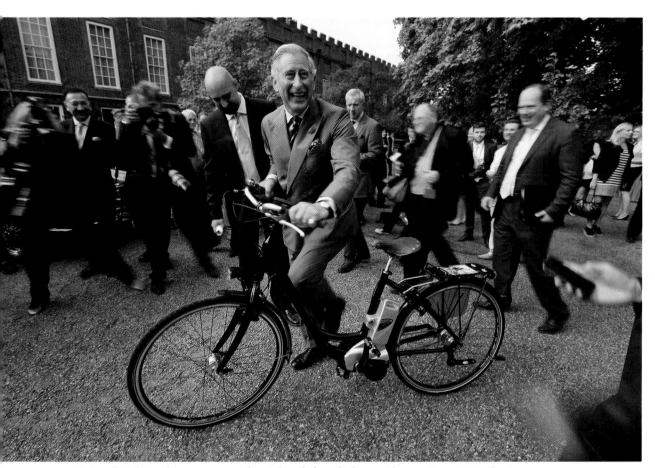

His Royal Highness demonstrates an electric bicycle for onlookers at Clarence House in London in 2011

Scenes From a Fairy Tale

Their marriage captivated global audiences and boosted British support for the monarchy. Its future rests in their hands

By William Lee Adams

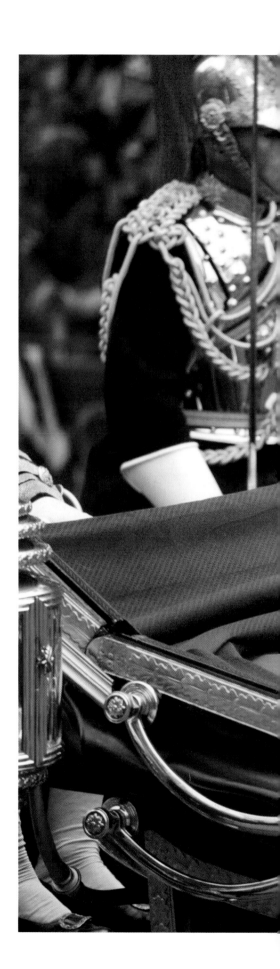

O n Nov. 16, 2010, just minutes after the announcement that Prince William would marry his longtime girlfriend Kate Middleton, British Prime Minister David Cameron delivered a statement of congratulations, helicopters circled Buckingham Palace, and news channels were looping footage of the young couple sharing intimate moments at a garden party. The nonstop chatter of royal watchers immediately followed, their discussions revolving around what Kate would wear down the aisle and whether that aisle would be in St. Paul's Cathedral, where William's parents, Prince Charles and Princess Diana, married 30 years earlier, or Westminster Abbey, which wouldn't raise the specter of his parents' drawn-out divorce.

Despite the glare of the media spotlight, 28-year-old Kate must have felt a degree of relief. On that day—after an eight-year courtship that had survived constant speculation, relentless pursuit by paparazzi, a high-profile breakup and an even higher-profile reconciliation—the royal family had finally made public what Kate had known or at least privately hoped

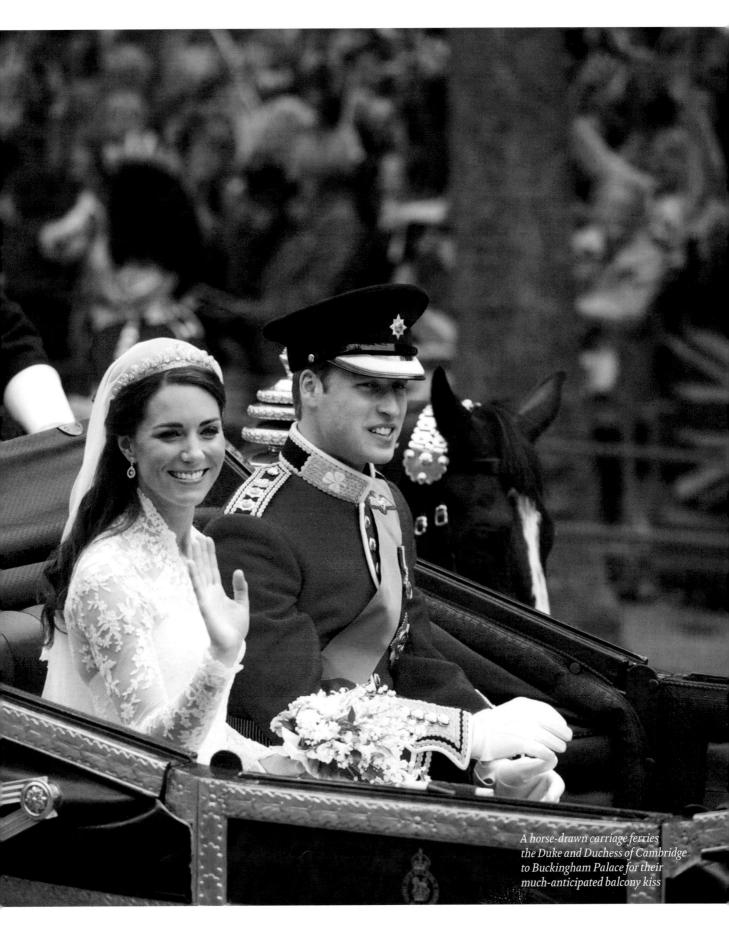

A horse-drawn carriage ferries the Duke and Duchess of Cambridge to Buckingham Palace for their much-anticipated balcony kiss

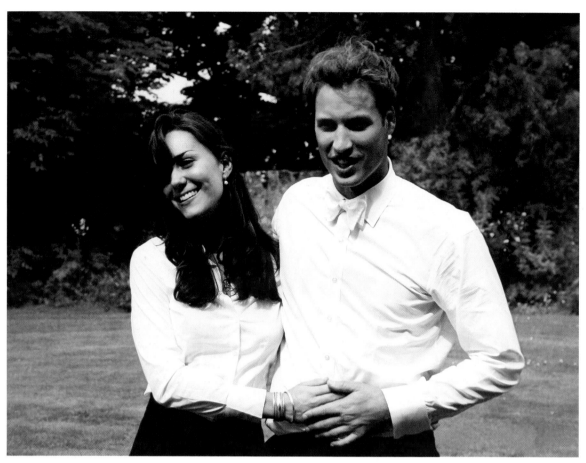

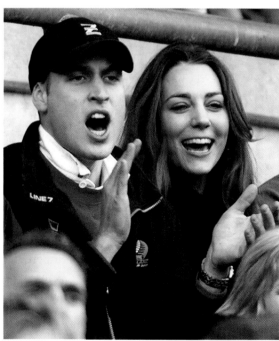

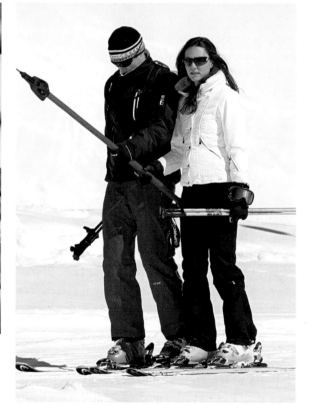

Their 2005 graduation from St. Andrews University (top), marked the end of their private romance. Paparazzi later snapped them at a rugby match outside London in 2007 and on a ski holiday in Klosters, Switzerland, in 2008

for years: The future king really had found his queen.

With that single announcement the royal constellation added a new star. Kate pulled an entire nation into her orbit, bewitching royal supporters, everyday Joes, and girls too young to spell her name. The international curiosity stemmed partly from the walls the royal family had erected around her. William, no doubt, wanted to protect his would-be bride from the media intrusion that some say robbed him of his other great love, his mother. Even so, in the months leading up to the April 29 wedding, the media brought an ever-slimmer Kate into sharper focus—not merely as the future Mrs. William Windsor, but also as a commoner who had risen to the apex of British society and a style maven who had launched a thousand knockoff dresses along the way.

By most accounts the wedding showcased Britain at its best. In a spectacular show of pomp and pageantry, austere Britain seemed, for a few hours, anyway, to throw off concerns about the economy, the euro and civil unrest (though rooftop snipers were in position to ward off the threat of terrorism). Rich and poor gathered on the streets outside Westminster Abbey and along the regal thoroughfares leading to Buckingham Palace, hoping for a glimpse of the horse-drawn carriage carrying the newlyweds toward their future. But Prince William and Kate—dubbed Catherine, Duchess of Cambridge, that morning—knew the spectacle afforded the public more than an afternoon of free entertainment and that it symbolized much more than the union of husband and wife. For the hundreds of millions of people around the world watching on TV and online, it was a reminder of monarchy's charm and unifying power. Yes, economic woe grips Britain. Public distrust of politicians is multiplying by the day. And millions of the royal subjects face a potentially less prosperous tomorrow. Yet in the year since their wedding, William and Kate have managed to burnish the Windsor family name. Whether visiting charities that work with homeless youth or walking the red carpet for the London premiere of *War Horse,* Mr. and Mrs. work as a team. "It's been a long while since Britons have had a young, good-looking couple to cheer about," says Robert Jobson, author of *William and Kate: The Love Story.* "It's certainly given the monarchy a younger, fresher feel—and a bit more relevance as a result."

The couple has managed to exhibit a common touch without sacrificing the mystique of royalty. While William, who turns 30 in June 2012, pursues his military career as a search-and-rescue pilot with the Royal Air Force, they've continued to live in a four-bedroom farmhouse on the island of Anglesey in North Wales. They've chosen not to employ a chef, butler or valet, and Kate has declined ladies-in-waiting. In February 2012, a royal aide revealed that William would like to extend his military service beyond mid-2013, when his current three-year commitment ends. That would limit the couple's public duties and allow them to start a family in relative privacy. "The appearance of normality makes people of their age able to connect with them," says *Debrett's Peerage and Baronetage* editor Charles Kidd. "That will inevitably change when the Queen's reign ends and the Prince of Wales succeeds. These are precious years."

The public successes the duke and duchess have racked up aren't put down merely to luck or the skilled hands of their choreographers. They stem from Kate and William's obvious strength as a couple. Long before they contemplated living as husband and wife, they navigated a long, occasionally tumultuous courtship. William was born into the firm. Kate has had a long apprenticeship.

A Royal Courtship

Catherine Elizabeth Middleton was born on Jan. 9, 1982, and grew up in the village of Bucklebury, population some 2,000. Strolling through Bucklebury Common—a sprawling, 900-acre park and the town's visual centerpiece—Kate's parents may have told their children about the park's royal legacy. Community leaders planted its inner ring of oak trees sometime in the 1560s to celebrate a visit by Queen Elizabeth I, and more trees were added in 1972, when Queen Elizabeth II toured the grounds. It's doubtful they interpreted them as signs of their eldest child's destiny.

The Middleton family's flight into the upper echelons of British society began at a British airport. Michael and Carole Middleton met in the 1970s working at British Airways—she as a flight attendant, he as a manager. They married in 1980, and the airline transferred Michael to Jordan four years later. Kate, then 2 years old, attended an English-language nursery school in Amman, and Carole stayed at home with 8-month old Philippa. Two-and-a half years later the Middletons returned to Bucklebury. In 1987,

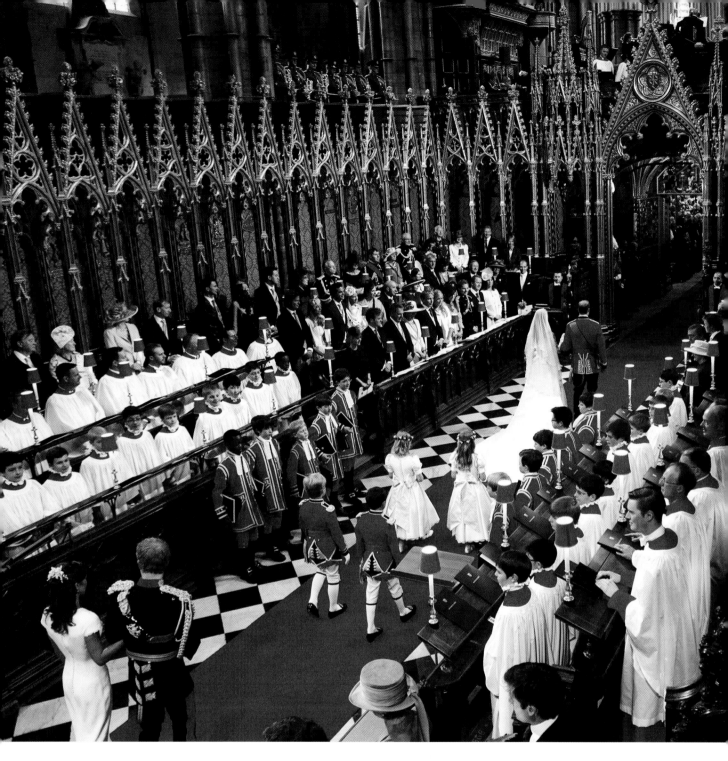

Carole gave birth to their youngest child, James.

That's when she had her multimillion-dollar idea. As a stay-at-home mom struggling to round up balloons and streamers for Kate's and Pippa's after-school parties, she decided to set up Party Pieces—a mail-order company selling children's party supplies such as kazoos and stuffed pigs. As the orders rolled in, the Middletons bought a five-bedroom house and expanded operations from a backyard shed to a series of converted farmhouses. The business, which analysts have estimated could be worth $48 million,

catapulted the family into a genteel world where aspirational women hunt wearing pearls.

It also allowed them to send their children to prestigious Marlborough College, a tony English boarding school that costs more than $48,000 a year and boasts alumnae that include Britain's first lady, Samantha Cameron. Kate didn't stand out for her academic ability, but she excelled as a leader and athlete, running circles around her classmates as a member of the field hockey and cross-country running teams.

Kate's decision to study at the University of St.

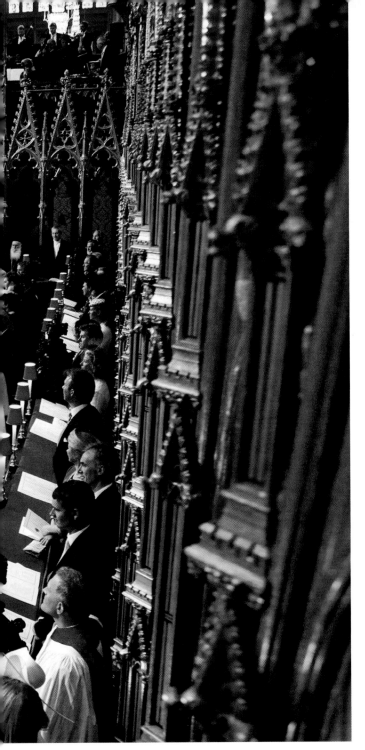

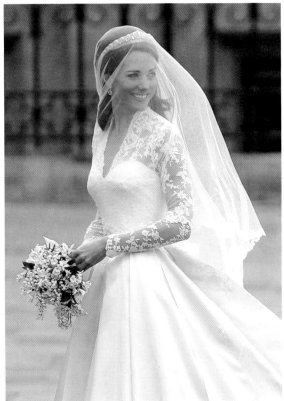

Andrews in Scotland fit with her family's rising ambitions. The school attracts scores of blue-blooded students from south of the Scottish border. That year it also attracted Prince William, who (like his future bride) chose to study art history there instead of pursuing a degree at Cambridge, as his father did. Shortly after his arrival, reporters suggested that many of his female classmates had already purchased wedding gowns. "I suppose they're saying that tongue-in-cheek," he responded. "But people who try to take advantage of me and get a piece of me—I spot it quickly and soon go off them."

The 19-year-old prince also knew how to spot a keeper—even one wearing just a bit of translucent clothing. He had become casual friends with Kate shortly after arriving on campus. During their second term, he paid $320 to support her at a charity fashion show. Kate sashayed down the runway wearing a see-through silk tube with a bandeau top and bikini bottom. She had a fuller figure than we know today and exhibited a degree of daring that will likely never reappear publicly. Photographers snapped a mesmerized William ogling. That fall, at the start of their second academic year, the two became housemates, along with two of their friends.

It's unclear when the friendship blossomed into something more. Buckingham Palace repeatedly denied a romance. Officials brokered a deal with the paparazzi that allowed William and Kate to grow their relationship in relative privacy in exchange for regular updates on his life. "There's been a lot of speculation about every single girl I'm with, and it actually does quite irritate me after a while, more so because it's a complete pain for the girls," William

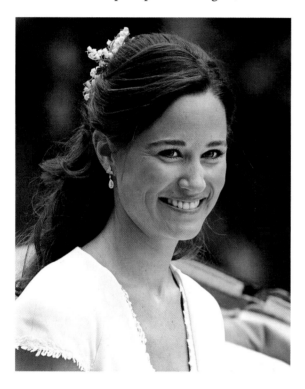

PIPPA MIDDLETON

Pippa—the middle Middleton—won the royal-wedding fashion stakes when she swayed into Westminster Abbey in a hip-hugging bridesmaid dress. Her pert figure became the subject of 60 tweets per minute and made her one of Google's fastest-growing search terms. In an online testimonial, she later credited her Pilates instructor for keeping her "fit, happy and energized." Now 28, Pippa edits the Party Times, *her family's web magazine, and works as an events planner in London. In November 2011 she reportedly secured a $640,000 deal to write a book on throwing the perfect party. Interest in Pippa isn't letting up. In January 2012, the photo editor of Britain's* Daily Mail *revealed that photographers send him up to 400 pictures of Pippa every day.*

said ahead of his 21st birthday. But in March 2004, a photo of the couple skiing in Switzerland finally exposed their relationship.

The cloak of security afforded them by the university couldn't last forever. In June 2005, graduation yanked it off entirely, and Kate had to face the media head-on. Issues of class quickly came to the fore, even before it became common knowledge that her family tree had branches held up by miners and manual laborers. Reporters claimed that William's well-heeled friends referred to Kate's mother with the flight-check phrase, "Doors to manual." Mean-spirited classmates even nicknamed Kate and Pippa, who studied at nearby Edinburgh University, the "wisteria sisters." The punch line? They're decorative and fragrant with a fierce ability to climb.

More worrying were the paparazzi who stalked Kate through the streets of London, publishing photos of her on the bus en route to a job interview and cycling to the gym in athletic shorts. The Palace provided Kate with 24-hour security through the Royal Protection Group (SO14), beginning in February 2006. Journalists gritted their teeth and kept up their occasionally lawless hunt for information. In January 2007, the former royal editor of the *News of the World* admitted to intercepting phone messages between William, Harry and their aides. He and his co-conspirator, a private investigator, served jail time.

The low point came in March when the couple split during a ski holiday in Switzerland. William reportedly wanted to enjoy the bachelor life while in the military. Rather than sulk at home, Kate decided to take to the town. Photographers snapped her looking glamorous and apparently unmoved by the snub from her wayward prince. Catherine Ostler, former editor of the high-society magazine *Tatler,* believes Kate's poise during that period ultimately boosted her popularity. "She came out of that breakup rather well," Ostler told TIME on the day the engagement was announced. "She went out, looked great, and eventually he went back with his tail between his legs. It made her look like the triumphant underdog."

Just two months after their split, the media started publishing reports of a reconciliation. Joint appearances in public—including at the July 2007 memorial concert for Princess Diana—confirmed

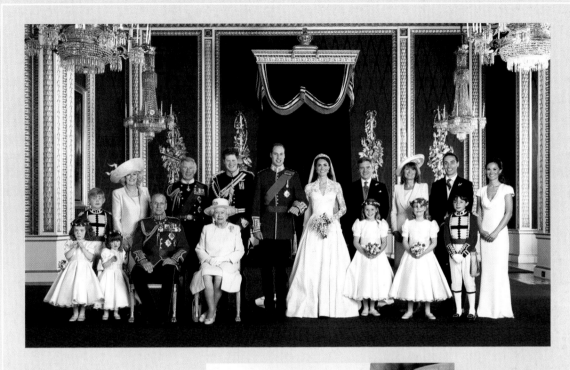

Kate's Coat of Arms

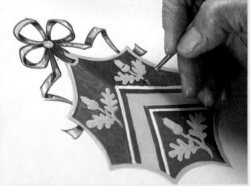

The Middletons posed for an official portrait with the royal family inside Buckingham Palace shortly after the wedding. At left, an artist draws a version of the Middleton coat of arms

Ahead of the royal wedding, Michael Middleton commissioned a family crest to mark his daughter's ascent from middle-class socialite to full-fledged royal.

For a fee of $7,040, an artist from London's College of Arms worked with the family to create the heraldic design. It's heavy with symbolism. Three acorns represent the three Middleton children and also reference the oak tree—a symbol of west Berkshire, where the family has lived for 30 years. The division down the middle of the crest plays on the Middleton family name, while the gold chevron invokes Carole Middleton's maiden name,

Goldsmith. The narrow white chevrons above and below the gold chevron reference mountain peaks, for the family's love of skiing and England's Lake District. The red and blue coloring helps distinguish the Middleton crest from a preexisting coat of arms dating back to the 16th century, which also features a chevron between three sprigs of oak.

The design comes in multiple forms. The version pictured above was printed on the back of the commemorative royal-wedding souvenir program.

Prince William's arms, which feature a shield supported by a lion and a unicorn, appeared on the front. While men use shields on personal heraldry, only women can carry this elaborate lozenge shape. The blue ribbon denotes a single woman: Pippa Middleton can still use this coat of arms, but married Kate cannot. After the wedding, artists erased the ribbon and inserted the resulting design into the center of her husband's. From heraldry to marriage, it really is a case of two becoming one.

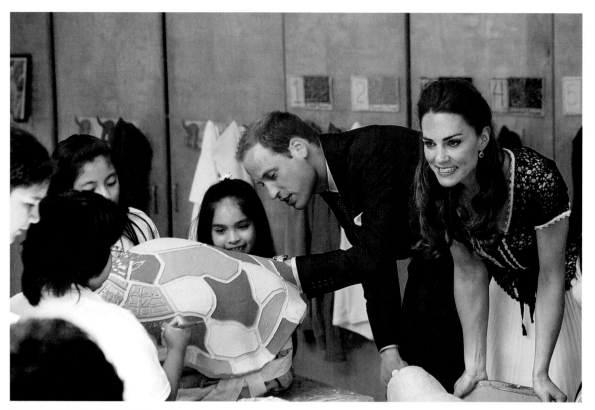

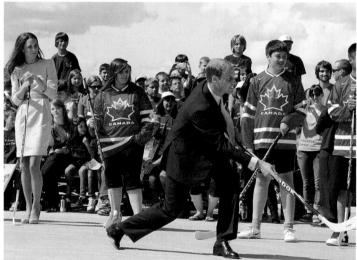

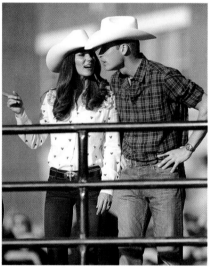

On their summer 2011 North American tour, the newlyweds made ceramics with inner-city kids in Los Angeles, donned cowboy hats at a Calgary, Alberta, rodeo and played road hockey in Yellowknife in the Northwest Territories

it. When the two hit the slopes in Klosters again in March 2008, the press wondered aloud when "Waity Katie" would get her proposal. It came in October 2010, during a 10-day safari in Kenya. William took Kate to the Rutundu Log Cabins, accessible only by air, horseback or a nine-mile walk from the nearest road. He carried his mother's sapphire engagement ring, now worth about $150,000, in his

backpack. "It was very romantic," Kate said in her first televised interview. "There's a true romantic in there. I really didn't expect it. It was a total shock ... and very exciting."

The Making of a Duchess

As royal-wedding fever spread across the world, Kate retreated into the cocoon of the royal estates. In January 2011, the Palace announced that Kate had left her part-time job at her parents' party business to "concentrate full-time on preparing to become a member of the royal family." Three decades earlier, Palace staff had assumed that Diana—who came from one of the country's oldest aristocratic families—could intuitively manage royal protocol and the anxiety of a dissected life, despite being just 20 years old. They couldn't have been more wrong: Diana suffered years of torment at the hands of the media before she learned to manipulate it. "The experience must have led the Palace to realize that a new bride in this very public role has to have care and training and a lot of backup," says *Debrett's* editor Kidd. "Catherine is of course from a very different background. This has sharpened everyone up a bit."

The eight-year courtship gave her a running start. Although she rarely appeared publicly in the lead-up to the wedding—she poured champagne on a new lifeboat in Wales in February and flipped pancakes in Belfast in March, both times alongside William—she seemed at ease. Crowds responded at every turn, partly because of Kate's million-dollar smile and willingness to engage with them, but also because of their own desire to be swept up in the romance.

On April 11, during her final public outing before the wedding, she and the Prince traveled to Darwen in Lancashire, a village 180 miles northwest of London, to open a school. As their motorcade pulled up, 2,000 well-wishers clapped and cheered despite the pouring rain. Kate emerged from her car wearing a navy-blue skirt suit and three-inch heels—and sheltering under a massive umbrella, which she carried herself. "She's just beautiful," Marion Riley, 57, told TIME after seeing Kate for just a few moments. "There could have been more guards around her, but she didn't want them. She went to shake hands, and she waved at everybody." Margaret Worthington, 71, seemed even more moved. "She really does appear a nice person," she said. "It brings tears to my eyes."

The duke and duchess chatted briefly with the Obamas at Buckingham Palace during their May 2011 state visit to Britain

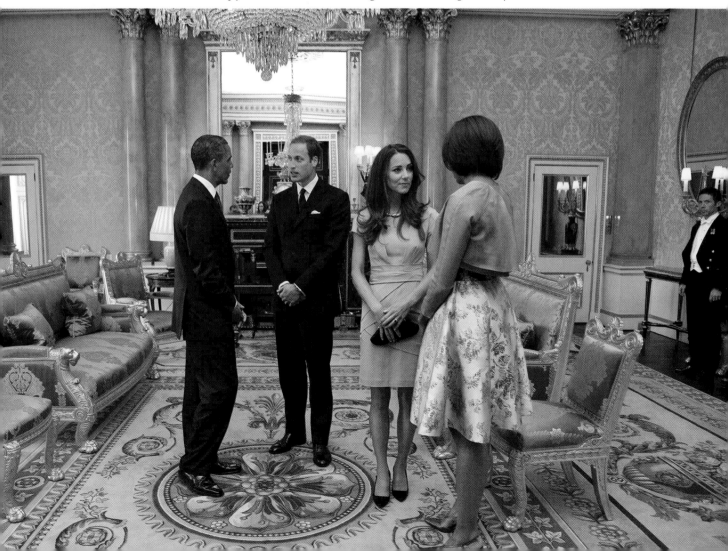

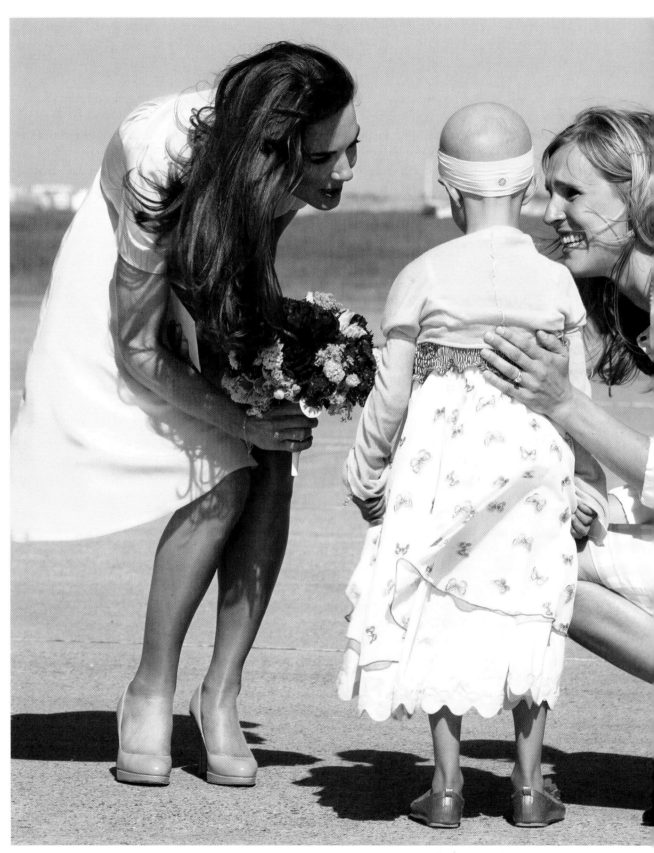

Crowds and journalists alike were impressed by Kate's ease with Diamond Marshall, a 6-year old with cancer, at the Calgary airport. "She told me she liked the flowers a lot," Diamond said after the encounter. "She was as fancy as she looks on the TV"

The next time the world would see Kate, she'd be wearing white.

On April 29, the wedding unfolded like a red carpet, rolling out smoothly from Westminster Abbey to Buckingham Palace and into the living rooms of viewers around the world. All the Queen's horses (well, 187 of them) and all the Queen's men (including 5,000 police officers) took their positions, and a million spectators flooded London's parks and sidewalks. At precisely 10:51 a.m., Kate and her father departed the nearby Goring Hotel. She smiled throughout the seven-minute journey and maintained a serene expression as she stepped onto the carpet outside the cathedral. Trailed by a 9-ft. ivory train, her sister and six young attendants, she made her way toward William.

Anyone—even a future king—can feel small beneath the towering spires of Westminster. During Kate's three-minute walk down the aisle, a nervous and slightly fidgety William bit his lip. "Wait till you see her," his best man, Prince Harry, told him. Kate arrived, and despite the grand setting, the gaze of onlookers and years of expectation, William leaned into her and whispered, "You look beautiful." It took lip-readers to deduce that for the press, but anyone watching got the message.

"That blend of formality with a relaxed atmosphere is something very special," says Richard Fitzwilliams, royal watcher and the former editor of *International Who's Who*. "People's spirits were uplifted with the knowledge that they seemed so at ease with one another and that the succession is now so secure." For months the royals had stressed the human dimensions of the wedding, including the fact that the father of the bride would contribute toward its costs. Because William is second in line to the throne, behind Prince Charles, the wedding was not an official state occasion, which gave William and Kate the freedom to make it their own. They didn't face pressure to invite heads of state like President Obama. Instead, they filled the aisles with schoolmates, representatives of their charities, and celebrities, notably Elton John, who had comforted Princess Diana during trying times. After their balcony kisses in the afternoon, they drove away from the palace in an Aston Martin decorated with balloons and a license plate that read JU5T WED. That evening they hosted an intimate afterparty inside Buckingham Palace.

Around 2:30 a.m. the DJ played the official last dance: "She Loves You" by the Beatles.

Beyond Westminster Abbey

The Duchess of Cambridge walked down the aisle a commoner and glided back up a royal. She looked calm, even joyful. If she was quivering beneath all the lace and flowers, we may never know. In the many public appearances she and William have made in the year since their wedding—mingling with Michelle and Barack Obama at Buckingham Palace during a state visit, painting at an inner-city arts school in Los Angeles—they appear stronger together than they do apart. But Kate—she of the perfectly coiffed hair and immaculately tailored gowns—hasn't yet given the world an opportunity to see the soul beneath the polished exterior. "I wouldn't say she's establishing an identity of her own just yet, because we haven't seen enough of her on her own," says writer Robert Jobson. "It's a conscious decision to present William and Kate as a team and a couple."

Occasionally there are glimpses of a rich inner life. In January the duchess announced the four charities she will support as an official patron. Two of them—the National Portrait Gallery in London and the Art Room, a charity that uses art as therapy for children—reflect a lifelong interest in the arts. Her choice of East Anglia's Children's Hospices, based in Cambridge, hints at her desire to make her role as Duchess of Cambridge more than titular. And, according to a Palace source, working with Action on Addiction, which helps children and families coping with substance abuse, reflects her observation that addiction is "at the heart of many of the social issues she was looking at." On Feb. 8, while William was deployed in the Falkland Islands, the duchess made her first solo appearance, at the Lucien Freud exhibition at the National Portrait Gallery. A week later she visited a Ronald McDonald house in Liverpool. On both occasions cameras flashed, the duchess smiled, and crowds cheered a woman standing on her own.

The true magic of Will and Kate may lie in the "and." Prince Charles and Diana seemed to recoil from one another in their engagement photographs, and throughout their marriage he resented that she overshadowed him. William, however, openly admires his wife and values her influence. As he said not long before their wedding, "She's got a really naughty sense of humor, which kind of helps me because I've got a really dry sense of humor." His public speaking engagements now seem less wooden, as if her glamour rubs off on him, giving him the confidence to speak straight from the heart. "She knows her task is to support him," says Fitzwilliams. "It isn't a competitive relationship. When they are together you see how strong the teamwork actually is."

It's an exportable commodity and one that will help them preserve the link between Crown and Commonwealth—the band of 54 independent countries that once made up the British Empire, 16 of which retain Queen Elizabeth as symbolic head of state. Polling data from May 2011 showed that 55% of Australians age 14 or older prefer to keep the monarchy—the highest level since 1991. In August, Canada quietly restored the "royal" prefix to the Royal Canadian Armed Forces.

More than any other event, the couple's 11-day tour of Canada and the U.S. in the summer of 2011 cemented faith in their ambassadorial abilities. Only 18 international journalists followed Queen Elizabeth II on her Canadian tour in 2010. Nearly 300 followed the duke and duchess in 2011. "It was a real rejuvenation of the monarchy in Canada," says Christina Blizzard, a Canadian journalist who trailed them for her book *Young Royals on Tour.* "And the crowds weren't just made up of traditional monarchists, who one would assume are older white people." Locals praised their patience: The military timing of the tour mattered less to Kate than giving high-fives to children. William managed to win over crowds in Quebec City—a bastion of republicanism—by delivering a speech in French.

The defining moment, however, came in Calgary, when the duke and duchess met a 6-year-old cancer patient on an airport runway. Diamond Marshall, whose mother had passed away from cancer four years earlier, had written to the Children's Wish Foundation asking to meet "Princess Kate." Wearing a pink hairband across her bald head, she presented the duchess with flowers and a friendship bracelet before diving into her arms. Kate seemed delighted, and Diamond broke into tears. "Kate didn't make the mistake of bending over Diamond. She got down and talked to her on her level," Blizzard says. "There were some very cynical journalists on that runway, but there wasn't a dry eye in sight."

Happily Ever After?

While Kate the commoner has helped make monarchy modern, she must soon embark on the most traditional role of any royal consort: producing and raising an heir. Both Queen Elizabeth and Princess Diana announced their pregnancies within six months of marriage, at the ages of 21 and 20, respectively. Kate, 30, surely has that on her mind.

The media is willing her on. In September 2011 an American tabloid claimed she was pregnant with twins. Buckingham Palace swiftly issued a denial. Denials, however, don't dampen the anticipation. Every movement she makes—from holding a clutch purse near her stomach to declining peanut paste while sampling a UNICEF food package in Denmark—is analyzed as a prospective sign that a new royal is on the way. For its February 2012 issue, *Tatler* magazine—the social bible for the horse-and-pony set—ran a cover story warning Kate what to expect if she becomes pregnant in 2012: "At the opening ceremony of the Olympic Games [in London] you are going to have to dig deep into your soul to find any enthusiasm," the magazine warns. "All you'll be able to think about is whether the baby is distressed by the sudden loud noise."

She won't, however, need to worry about the gender of her first child. In October 2011, Commonwealth leaders unanimously agreed to change the Act of Succession, which for 300 years has dictated that the English crown pass to the oldest male heir, even if he has an older sister. "Put simply, if the Duke and Duchess of Cambridge were to have a little girl, that girl would one day be our queen," British Prime Minister David Cameron explained. Cameron said the previous arrangement was "at odds with the modern countries that we have become."

That suggests, rightly, that Britain's royals exist not merely to influence the values of their countrymen but also to reflect them. Prince William's heir, whoever he—or she—may be, will enter a family where a commoner can become queen and a prince can marry for love, where the crown worn by one is held up by many. Children will come in time. For now, William and Kate can rest assured that the next chapter of Windsor history is already written.

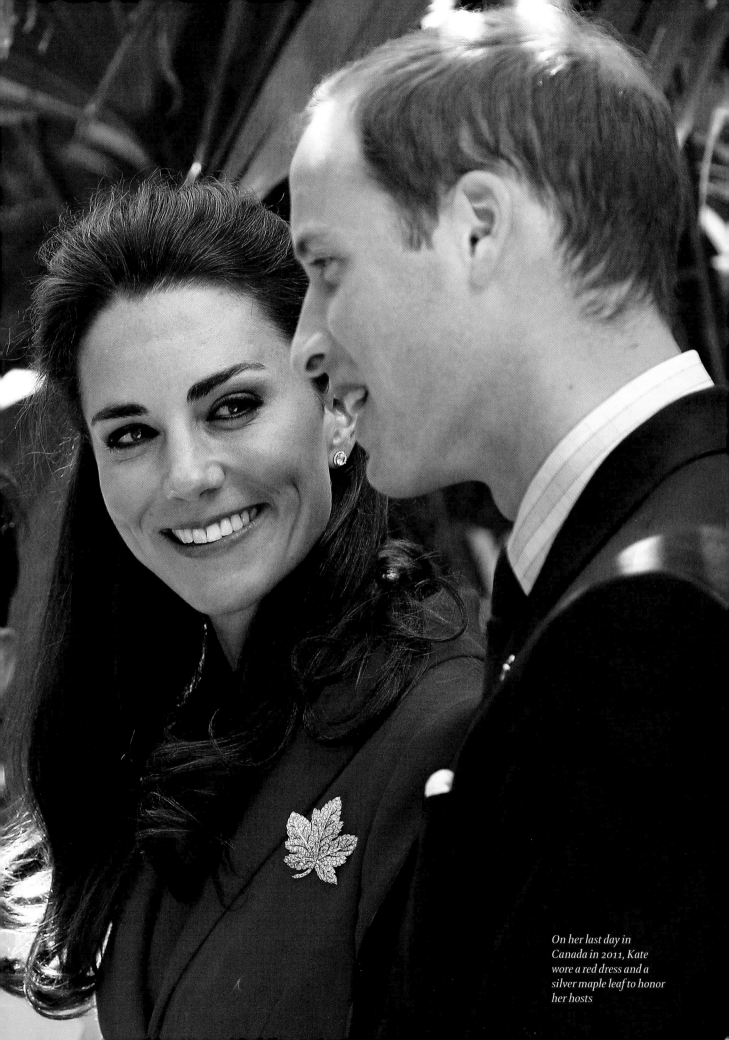

On her last day in Canada in 2011, Kate wore a red dress and a silver maple leaf to honor her hosts

All Grown Up Now

Long considered the royal wild child, he has found a calling in the military and in global charity—and has rehabilitated his image along the way

By William Lee Adams

I n February 2012, Capt. Harry Wales stepped onto a tiny stage in a private club in London and commanded attention far beyond his service rank. As patron of Walking with the Wounded, a charity that raises money for the reeducation of injured military veterans, Prince Harry had come to launch the group's 2012 expedition, which will see five former soldiers—some with missing limbs, others with severe burns—attempt to scale Mount Everest. He listened intently as, one by one, the men described surviving gunshot wounds, shattered femurs and amputations. When he delivered his own speech, his shaking arms and cracking voice conveyed nerves—and the extent to which their stories had stirred him. "They have given their all for our security. Security is the very least, as a nation, we owe them," he said, interrupted by the staccato snaps of flashing cameras. Mount Everest instills fear in the hearts of even seasoned mountaineers, he said, yet "not so for this crop of lunatics

with odd numbers of arms and legs, but staggering determination."

The 27-year-old unguarded foil to his buttoned-up brother—Harry foolishly wore a Nazi uniform to a costume party in 2005—was written off by his detractors for a time. But in recent years Harry has dealt his critics a firm rebuke. From fighting on the frontlines in Afghanistan in 2007-8 to training so he can redeploy to the war zone as an Apache helicopter pilot, he has proven himself a man of stout heart, not merely one given to late-night revelry. His changed image comes with age and his handlers' coaching, but it's also a result of Harry focusing his energy and pluck on something worthwhile. "The happiest time of his life was when he was on the frontlines," says Katie Nicholl, the author of *William and Harry*, an account of the Princes' lives. "It marked a sharp and clear transition between being a boy and being a man."

The journey began in his older brother's shadow. Despite Princess Diana's efforts to raise the boys as equals, Harry struggled with his role as William's

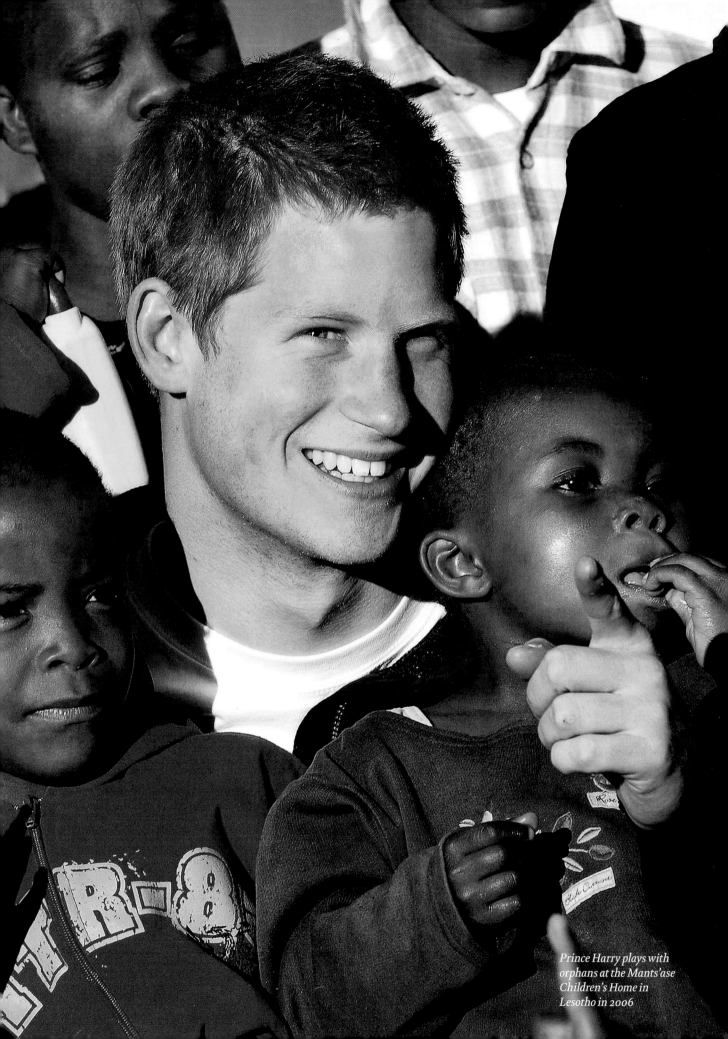

Prince Harry plays with orphans at the Mants'ase Children's Home in Lesotho in 2006

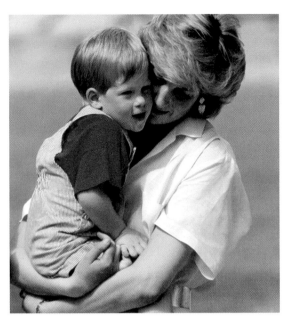

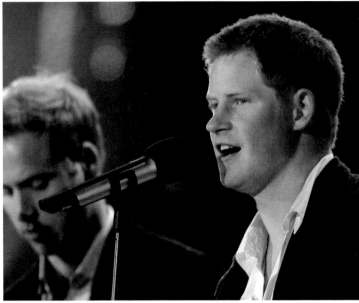

Prince Harry (with Princess Diana, above) delivered a moving tribute to his mother at the 2007 Concert for Diana (right), which marked the 10th anniversary of her death. Below, on the frontlines in Afghanistan in 2008

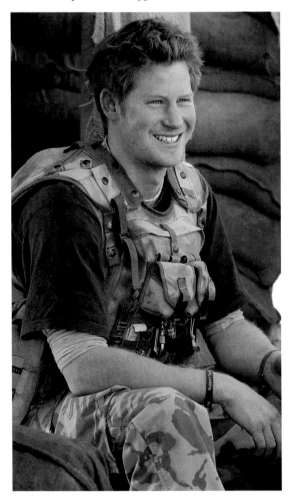

backup. According to Ingrid Seward, editor of *Majesty* magazine, the Queen Mother paid less heed to Harry than to his brother. "Harry felt all the attention was on William," she says. "He sort of felt like a bit of an also-ran." At Eton, the prestigious boarding school both boys attended, he once again found himself the royal afterthought. William didn't exactly excel academically, but Harry lagged behind him; his achievements were limited to sports and his role as class clown. It appeared at times that he sought to define himself in contrast to squeaky-clean William. In 2001, Prince Charles sent 16-year-old Harry to a rehab clinic for a day after he admitted to drinking and smoking pot near the family home in Highgrove. "This is a serious matter which was resolved within the family and is now in the past and closed," officials at St. James's Palace said.

The Princes, however, have always been close. They depended on one another as they faced the strain of their parents' high-profile divorce and the tragedy of losing their mother. In the days following Diana's car crash, photographers captured William, then 15, looking tenderly at grieving Harry, 12. At Eton, Harry, cheeky like his mother, helped the more serious William relax. Once, when he was 15, Harry jumped out from behind a tree to startle William during a cross-country race. That rascally form of affection continues today. In April 2011, Harry served as William's best man at the royal wedding. "As far as I was concerned, I was there to support him, to tell him how great he is," Harry said later in a BBC documentary. "Obviously it was his day, so I had to lie."

Harry came into his own when he enrolled at Sandhurst, Britain's elite military academy, in 2005. In uniform, his royal credentials mattered little, and he could live as one of the boys. That September, in a wide-ranging interview to mark his 21st birthday, he made it clear that he wanted to serve in Iraq. But in May 2007, the military announced it wouldn't deploy him, fearing he would become a prime target. Seven months later, however, Harry got the all-clear after the British media agreed to keep his deployment a secret. He arrived in southern Afghanistan on Dec. 14, the first royal to serve in a war zone since Prince Andrew piloted helicopters during the Falklands War in 1982. Operating near Taliban positions, Harry patrolled hostile areas, oversaw air strikes, and endured regular attacks from rocket-propelled grenades. Strangely, war brought Harry a degree of peace with himself. As he confided to a reporter embedded with his unit: "I think this is about as normal as I'm ever going to get."

His tour of duty came to an abrupt end 10 weeks later when international media disclosed his whereabouts. The military withdrew him from the field, fearing his presence threatened the safety of his comrades. The same down-market tabloids that previously dismissed him as a party animal now praised him as a war hero. In an article headlined "When Harry Met Tali," the *Daily Star* wrote that he "dodged bullets to defy danger and blast away at the enemy for Gran and country."

But winning over the media mattered less to Harry than getting back to the action. Learning to fly was the fastest way, because a prince would be considered less vulnerable in the air. In February 2012 he concluded 18 months of intense training that will allow him to man the Apache—the $74 million attack helicopter. It's a remarkable achievement: Fewer than one in 10 who apply qualify for the elite squadron. Harry graduated at the top of his class of more than 20 airmen and could see combat by the end of 2012.

Harry's transformation has won him the confidence of Her Majesty, who dispatched him to the Caribbean on his first solo overseas tour as a representative of the Crown to mark her Diamond Jubilee. Previous trips abroad have showcased his compassion. Like his mother, Harry can put even the most desperate children at ease, as he has shown with his charity Sentebale, which works on behalf of AIDS orphans and other vulnerable children in Lesotho. In 2004 he cradled a 10-month-old girl who had been raped by her HIV-positive stepfather—and looked close to tears as he heard her story. "I held her in my arms," he said in a documentary filmed at the time. "She couldn't move. She had no expression. No laughing, no crying."

His willingness to engage with his emotions in public defies Windsor culture. It may stem from losing his mother early in life. The image of forlorn Harry, his head down, on the day of Diana's funeral, touched the nation—as did the letter addressed to "Mummy" he placed on her coffin. Few were surprised that Harry, not William, gave the tribute at the memorial concert marking the 10th anniversary of Diana's death. He wrote the speech himself. "She was quite simply the best mother in the world," he said. "She made us and so many other people happy. May this be the way that she is remembered."

Such heartfelt honesty—coupled with the fact that William is off the market—has made Harry Britain's most eligible bachelor. "Most of us royal hacks like him more than William," says Judy Wade, the royal correspondent for British celebrity magazine *Hello!* "As William grows balder and more nerdy with his old-fashioned spectacles, Harry gets more gorgeous." Chelsy Davy—who dated Prince Harry on and off from 2004 until 2011—already knew that. She stood next to him as he received his military wings and accompanied him to the royal wedding. But they split—seemingly for good—afterwards.

Though he once felt slighted by the focus on his brother, surely Harry now appreciates the freedom that comes with distance from the throne. William must live his life knowing he will one day be king and is expected to produce an heir. Harry, on the other hand, has more opportunity to rack up life experiences of his own choosing. "He's got all the perks without all the responsibilities," says Seward. "I think life is still a very big adventure for Harry." Unencumbered by a coming crown, Prince Harry has the audacity to envision a life outside of St. James's Palace. "I want to live in Africa and become a wildlife photographer," he told orphans in Lesotho in 2010. Given his knack for reinvention, he just might.

Diana's Enduring Spell

*She broke the Windsor code in revealing her
inner turmoil. In so doing, she changed Britain*

By Catherine Mayer

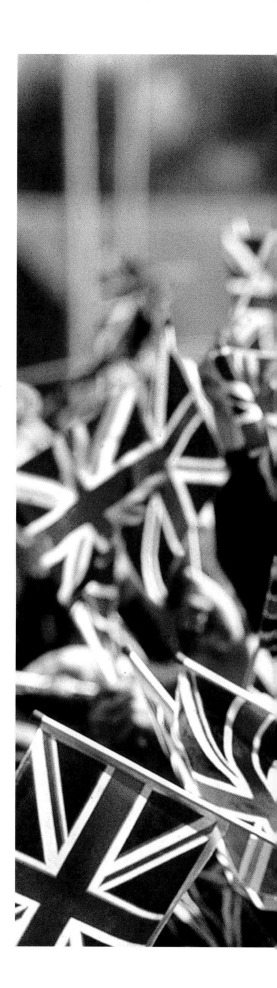

T he British have always been good at silence—at family meals spent wordlessly;
intense emotions expressed through a hand
on the shoulder—but on Sept. 6, 1997, they
surpassed themselves. London, the big,
braying capital, was stilled as an estimated
3 million mourners kept vigil along the
route to Westminster Abbey. The hush amplified the sounds
of the funeral cortège as it set out from Kensington Palace: the
rumble of wheels on tarmac, the clopping of horses' hooves,
a bell that tolled at listless intervals. But as the procession
came into view, turning out of the palace gates onto the
public road, a shriek pierced the morning air—"Diana, my
Diana!"—and then a despairing wail: "We love you, Diana!"
Britain's customary stoicism had been overwhelmed by raw,
unbridled grief.

It has become commonplace since the death of Diana,
Princess of Wales, to say that the festival of mourning which
culminated in her extraordinary funeral marked a transformation, the moment when the old British virtues of reserve and
silent suffering, of "mustn't grumble" and "could be worse,"

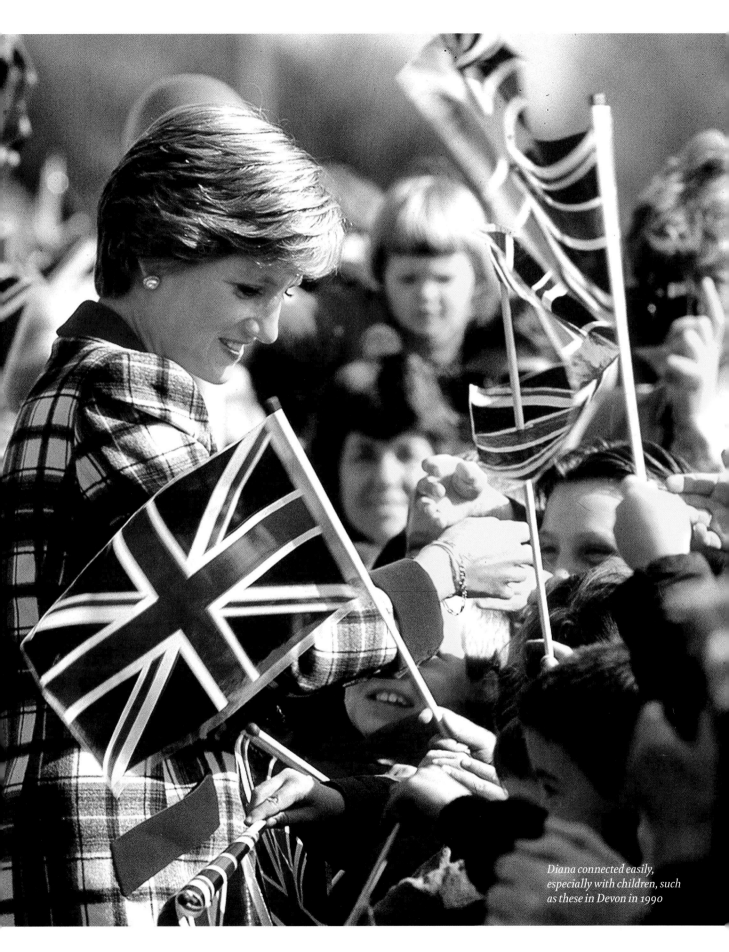

Diana connected easily, especially with children, such as these in Devon in 1990

gave way to publicly expressed catharsis. The People's Princess had unlocked hearts, reordered values, presided at the triumph of emotional intelligence over cold intellect, of compassion over tradition.

Three separate inquiries into the car crash in Paris that killed her at the age of 36 have concluded that it was precisely what it seemed to be at the time: a tragic accident. But the truth about Diana's life is harder to pin down, as tricky as the Princess herself could be. Diana's significance rests in a series of interlocking social and political revolutions in a nation with a disproportionate impact on global culture high and low —revolutions in which she participated, part unwitting catalyst, part canny activist.

The arrival of a new princess in the Windsor fold has again focused attention on Diana. But the obsession with measuring Kate against Diana to see how well she fits into the gap Diana left misses the point. There is no need or room for a replica Diana, because Diana's role—and legacy—was to change Britain and its monarchy.

That may sound overblown. And it's true that just as Diana was often underestimated in life, her achievements are frequently hyperbolized in death. But her influence is undeniable. Diana helped tear down prejudices about AIDS. She raised awareness of eating disorders. She coalesced opposition to land mines. These are pretty hefty achievements for a woman of little education who once sought to set a nervous child at ease by describing herself as "thick as a plank." Add to these a more dubious accomplishment—her skillful manipulation of media images—and it's clear why Diana remains an inescapable presence in British life, mostly, but not always, benign. A restless and seductive ghost, she still haunts many corners, not least in the drafty palaces that were once her habitat.

Modernizing the Monarchy

When a journalist asked Charles if he was in love with his 19-year-old fiancé, he churlishly replied, "whatever 'in love' means." Yet the Windsors thought they knew about love. It looked like patriotism. It was respectful and waved flags. It didn't sob on the streets or scream like a teenage girl glimpsing her rock idol. The British people hold the Queen in quiet affection.

Of course, there has always been dissent: An average 18% of Britons have called for the abolition of the monarchy since MORI, a polling firm, first began gathering opinions on the royals in 1969. That figure seemed as impervious to change as the Queen's fashion sense. Then Diana died, and for one week, republican numbers swelled to 25%.

The Queen's no-interview policy has helped to preserve the fraying mystique of royalty. But as her subjects wept on the streets and dying flowers carpeted the sidewalks, Elizabeth's Trappist vow looked either boneheaded or stone-hearted. Dickie Arbiter, a former press secretary to the Queen, Charles and Diana, who was responsible for the media arrangements for Diana's funeral, says it was neither. "The Queen was always going to pay tribute to Diana," he says, but she planned from the outset to make her broadcast shortly before the funeral. "There was a furor because she was at Balmoral and not down with the sniveling mobs in London. [But] William and Harry needed her more than hundreds and thousands of people keeping Kleenex in business."

Yet while the Queen and her immediate family kept their grief to themselves, there was a whiff of revolution beyond the palace gates. The U.S. academic Camille Paglia, speaking two days after the Paris car crash, predicted the fall of the House of Windsor. "With its acquisition of Diana, the monarchy had restored its modernity," she told Salon.com. "Instead its treatment—its mistreatment—of her ... may mean the end of the monarchy."

Not so. The Queen responded to the message of the MORI poll, and as soon as she walked among the mourners, support for ditching her plunged to historic lows. It was as if Britons had peered into the abyss of republicanism and drawn back in horror. The royals had learned a lesson, too, says Robert Worcester, MORI's founder: "The monarchy realized that it stands or falls on public opinion." Her children also took stock and decided that they had better justify their existence to the outside world.

Granted, not all of them have succeeded, and their options for doing so are limited to a narrow range of occupations, symbolic roles and good works. In the last of these categories, Diana set a standard that's hard to equal. She ignored the prevailing prejudices

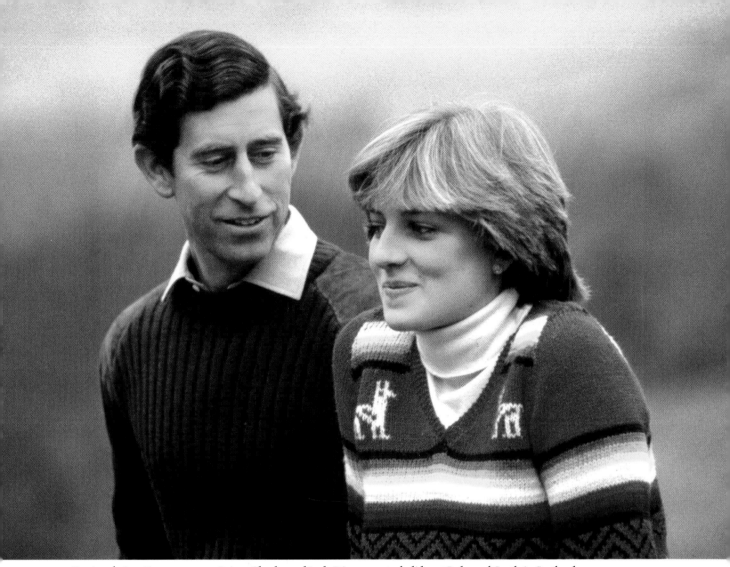

During their 1981 engagement, Prince Charles and Lady Diana spent a holiday at Balmoral Castle in Scotland

and fears about AIDS to clasp the hands of sufferers; she embraced leprosy patients in Indonesia. Arbiter remembers a visit to a home for the blind where Diana noticed that an elderly resident was crying. "She asked what was the matter, and he said, 'I can't see you.' So she took his hand and put it on her face." Charles still doesn't wear his heart on his sleeve, but he has emerged as an effective social entrepreneur.

In other ways, too, Diana lives on in her family. Charles visibly stepped up to the task of rearing their boys, not in the model of his own austere upbringing, but just as the Princess would have wanted. Their coming of age in the public eye wasn't without bumps and hiccups, but William, with Kate at his side, seems equable about his destiny, and Harry's navigation of the awkward nonrole of a younger royal sibling has been eased by more than a dash of Dianaesque charm.

If either prince resented Camilla, the longtime lover who helped to undermine their parents' flawed union, the emotion dissipated as they saw their father flourish in his second marriage. His visible contentment has also helped to turn around public opinion, once set firmly against Camilla. When, just before Diana died, MORI asked in a poll if Camilla should become queen, only 15% supported the idea. Ten years later that figure had swelled to 38%. Pollsters haven't since posed the question, but benign newspaper coverage and the warm responses her public appearances generate indicate that her stock has continued to rise among Britons. It is no small irony that ideas the Princess popularized—the pursuit of personal happiness, compassion for human weaknesses—have helped the cause of a woman she detested.

Unbuttoning Britain

Diana was brought up in about as old-fashioned an environment as was possible in the last quarter of

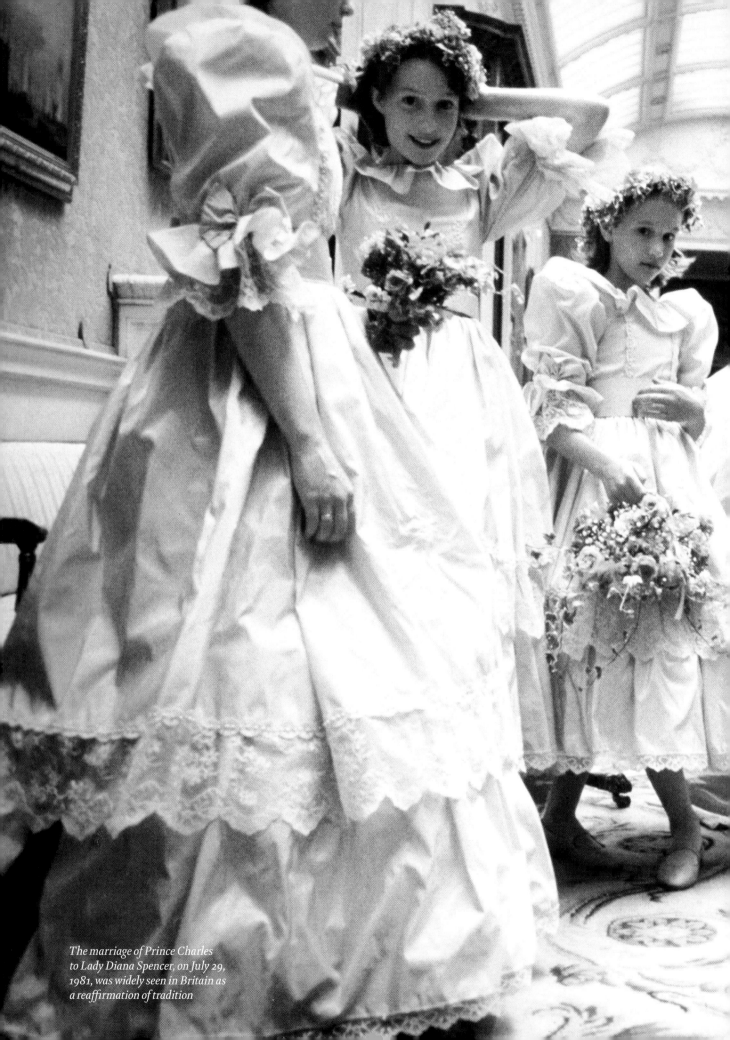

The marriage of Prince Charles to Lady Diana Spencer, on July 29, 1981, was widely seen in Britain as a reaffirmation of tradition

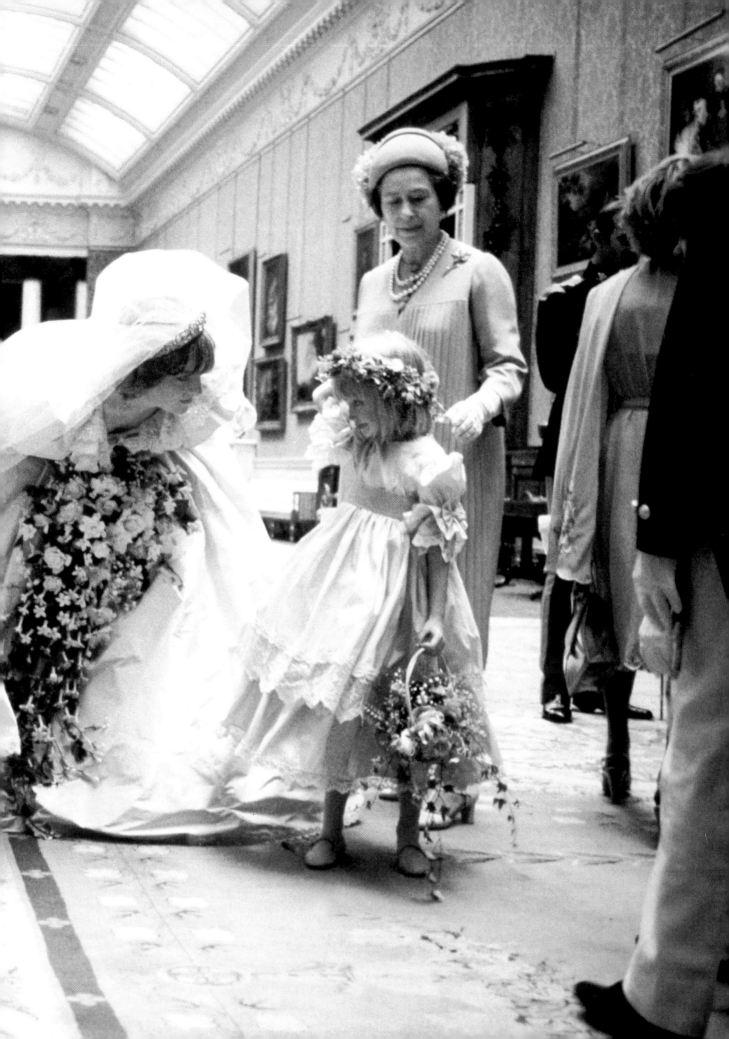

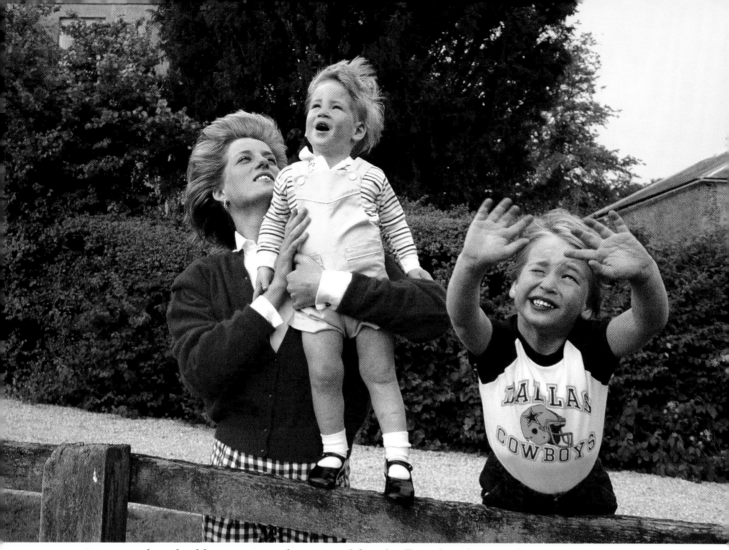

Diana was a devoted and demonstrative mother to Harry (left) and William, shown here at Highgrove House in 1986

the 20th century, but nothing could have prepared her for the antiquity of palace life. Britain had been post-imperial for more than a generation, which meant that the values associated with empire (or with its rulers) had long lost their edge. By the time she married, it was already—especially in London— a place less homogeneous, more multicolored than it had ever been, and far less deferential to the Victorian virtues that the royal family represented. Yet in the royal household, those virtues—and that deference—held sway. The new Princess could not fit in. Her rebellion, inchoate and self-destructive at first, reverberated far beyond the palace walls. Tina Brown, one of Diana's many biographers, relates asking former Prime Minister Tony Blair if Diana had found a new way to be royal. "No," Blair replied. "Diana taught us a new way to be British."

Blair's Labour party—New Labour, as it rechristened itself on the road to power—had been given power by electors who were reviewing their values. After the brash, moneymaking 1980s came the hangover of the early 1990s. Britons were searching for spiritual and emotional succor. That didn't make them deep. They set increasing store by celebrity. Success was measured by the ability to find fulfillment. It was a confessional age. Even before the country convulsed in grief for its lost Princess, Brits were eager to let it all hang out—at least by comparison with their grandparents and great-grandparents. If you doubt that, consider this passage in *The Ascent of Everest,* the account of the first conquest of the mountain in 1953, by John Hunt, who led the expedition. Hunt is describing the return of Edmund Hillary and Tenzing Norgay to camp after summiting. "Everyone was pouring out of the tents, there were shouts of exclamation and joy. The next moment I was with them: handshakes—even, I blush to say, hugs—for the triumphant pair."

Diana led the charge for emotion and the unembarrassed displays that now routinely go with it, from hugs and kisses to public tears. Unlike her remote royal in-laws, she touched the people she met, literally touched them, and bought their trust with a coinage she had in endless supply: her most personal thoughts and feelings. That's partly because her unhappiness drove her humanitarian impulses. Arbiter says, "She always championed the downtrodden" because she was attracted to their suffering. "She was a bit of an ambulance chaser, with the best of intentions." She also experimented with different therapies that encouraged her to unburden, if not necessarily in public. The comedian and writer David Baddiel, whose novel *Whatever Love Means* begins on the day of Diana's funeral, sees her as an exponent of "a degraded version of therapy culture," a self-help addict who couldn't stop spilling her guts. She "didn't know who she was but gained an identity through her messiness, through her lack of identity, by splattering her lack of identity on the walls of our culture," he says. "People chimed with that."

After her separation and divorce, Diana's efforts to redefine herself took on an edge of urgency. She had given up her patronage of most of the charities she once represented. She fantasized about becoming the wife of one of her boyfriends, a heart surgeon named Hasnat Khan, and living in anonymity.

Yet she could never hope to become normal. Instead she became a celebrity. Then came Dodi Fayed.

Though friends say he was just a distraction, her choice of two Muslim boyfriends looked set to test how deep the tolerance of New Labour's Britain would go. This much is plain: She had long since shed the attitudes of many white Britons.

Wayne Sleep, a ballet dancer and media personality, got to know Diana well and remembers her "poking fun at aristocracy." In her final years, she mingled less and less with her own class, preferring instead the company of the self-made aristocracy of entertainment and fashion. The members of this elite were from different countries and cultures—gay, straight, black, white—and were united by fame. In Blair's Britain, they could expect invitations to 10 Downing Street, not always because of their talent. (Britain may have shrugged off its forelock-tugging subservience to the ruling classes, but in Cool Britannia, money and celebrity counted.) Diana fit into this new world perfectly. She wasn't seen as posh; she was one of the people. By example, she reassured them that anyone could be a star. All you needed, she seemed to imply, was the chance to display yourself to the world. After all, she'd done that more than once

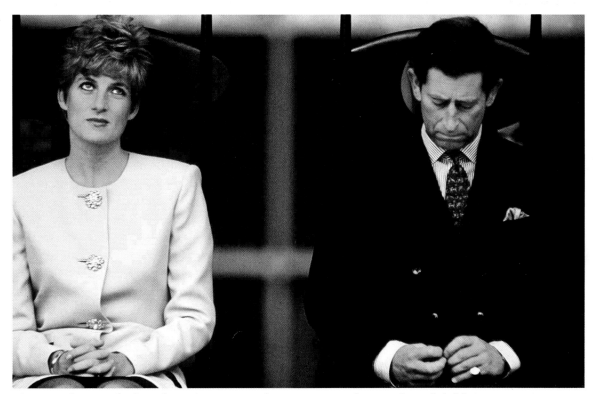

The tension between Charles and Diana was apparent during a 1991 Canadian tour that included their sons

herself. In 1985, at a gala evening to celebrate Charles' 37th birthday, she left the royal box and appeared on-stage, shimmying with Sleep. Charles was appalled. Diana's scheme to please him may have come undone, but she had helped Britain to unbutton.

From Fairy Tale to Post-Feminist

Imagine this: Diana is still alive. She's a well-preserved fiftysomething, with a series of boyfriends behind her and an apartment in Manhattan. Is she popular? Maybe. A legend? No way. By dying young, Diana ensured her immortality. Better dead than wrinkled or lifted.

Celebrity culture is cruel, especially to women. "One of the characteristics of celebrity culture is that you first build someone up, and then you write about their downfall," says German writer Tom Levine, the author of a book on Britain's first family (its title—*Die Windsors*—tends to startle English speakers). "If Diana had lived she would have been going on that up-and-down train."

Her last summer was already something of a downward ride. A slight weight gain set the press speculating she might be pregnant. She wasn't, and such close attention could not have been easy for a bulimic. But her public admission of her eating disorder in a 1995 interview with Martin Bashir for the BBC had encouraged hidden sufferers to seek help. Her life reflected many of the concerns of ordinary women—their weight, their relationship troubles—and by talking openly she also eroded the stigma attached to failure. Even a princess battled the bulge, even a beauty lost her husband. That may not seem dramatic by today's standards, but for the time and within the context of the stuffy establishment, it was "very radical," says feminist writer Naomi Wolf. Diana "didn't just talk the talk, she walked the walk."

That was not the fate feminists predicted when the news of her engagement to Charles broke. The feminist magazine *Spare Rib* ran an article headed "DON'T DO IT DI." This slogan, rendered as a lapel button, became a fashionable accessory for the thinking woman. "On 29 July 1981," wrote the British journalist Beatrix Campbell of the fairy-tale wedding in St. Paul's Cathedral, "the deceitful and depressed engagement ended when this thin, wan, whiter-than-white woman walked down the aisle, propping up the aged patriarch who had got her into

all this.... Her ivory silk wedding dress was a shroud."

By the time Diana died, however, many feminists had read her struggle against a sclerotic system as a parable of empowerment. Paglia dubbed her an "incredible superstar." That she was, but she would never have located herself in the feminist firmament. She wasn't interested in gender equality. She fought against a patriarchy because it was old-fashioned and restrictive, not because she repudiated its male values. The Princess was one of the first and most potent symbols of the "girl power" celebrated by the 1990s British pop sensation the Spice Girls, with their mildly predatory allure and celebration of girly friendship. It was a neat fit for Diana, with her close women friends and her troubled search for a mate. What Royal Spice really, really wanted was not at all radical: to love and be loved.

The Political Princess

Diana's body was transported to Westminster Abbey on a gun carriage. Arbiter says that's a detail of Diana's funeral that troubled Blair's communications chief, Alastair Campbell, and his team. The vehicle had been chosen because, unlike a hearse, it would be open to the crowds. To the Palace it also seemed appropriate: Diana had, after all, been the honorary colonel-in-chief of six regiments.

Yet Diana's last, passionate campaign was distinctly pacifist: She called for the abolition of land mines. She had visited Angola with the British Red Cross in January 1997, angering some Conservative MPs, who thought she was showboating. Said Peter Viggers, a Tory member of the Commons Defence Select Committee: "This is an important, sophisticated argument. It doesn't help simply to point at the amputees and say how terrible it is." Undaunted, Diana spoke at a conference on land mines and made a second fact-finding trip, to Bosnia.

Few would have predicted such engagement from the plummy girl who emerged on the public stage in 1980 as Charles' latest squeeze. The royal wedding in 1981—with Diana's endless train, the pages and flower girls, the choirs and coaches—was widely seen at the time as a reaffirmation of tradition in Britain, a throwback to an age when nobility and pomp held the nation in thrall. That it should have taken place during Margaret Thatcher's first term only added to the idea that Britain was becoming a more conserva-

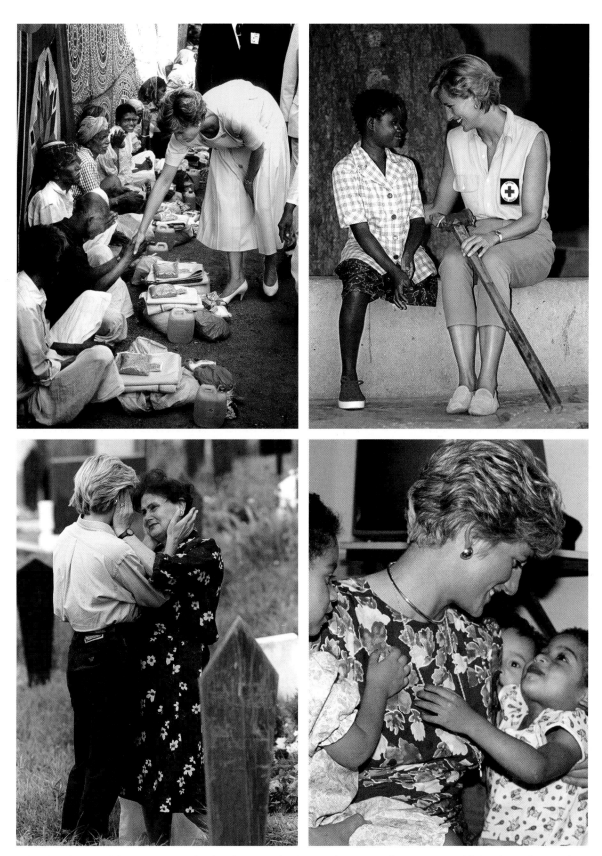

Clockwise from top left: The Princess touches the untouchables in India, 1992; talks to a 13-year-old Angolan girl injured by land mines, 1997; holds ill and abandoned babies in Brazil, 1991; and comforts a Bosnian war widow in 1997

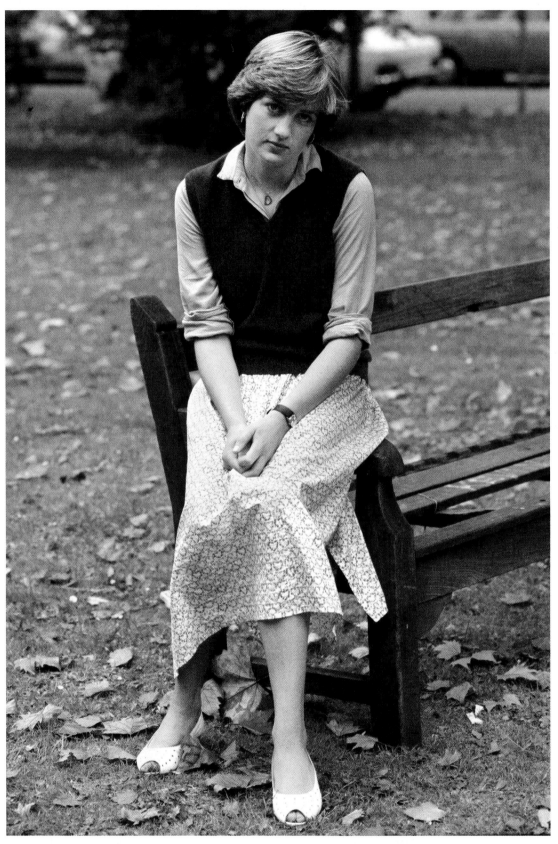

As the world watched, Lady Diana Spencer transformed from Shy Di, a 19-year-old nursery-school assistant (left, in 1980), to Diana, Princess of Wales, one of the world's most glamorous and admired celebrities (right, in 1996)

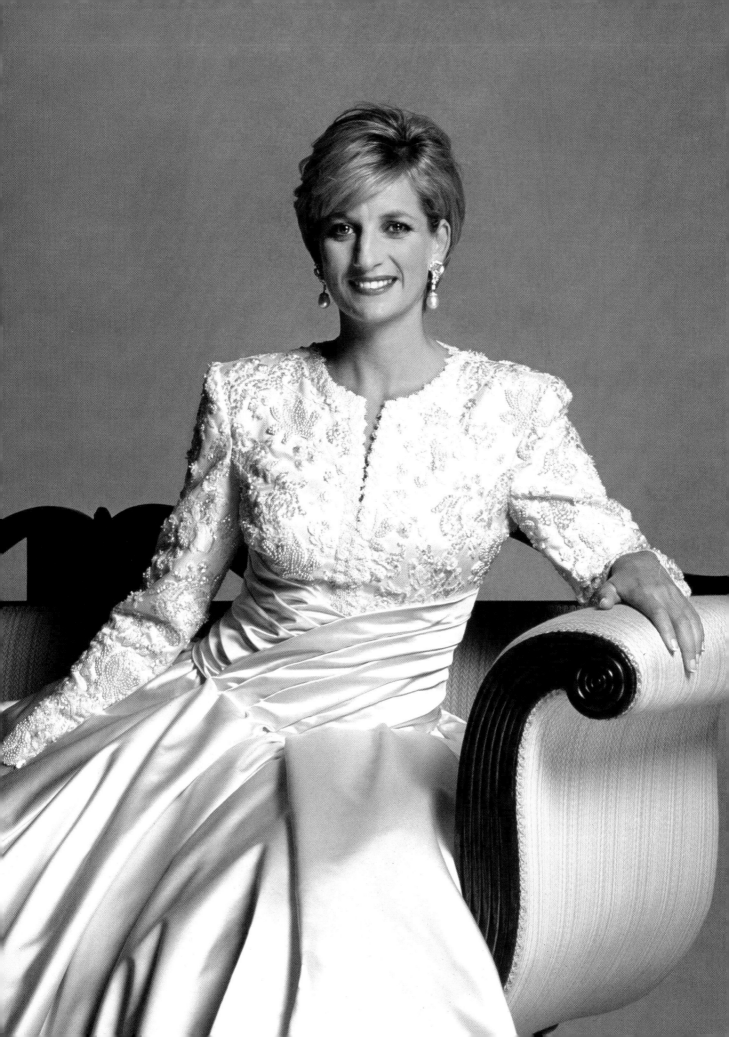

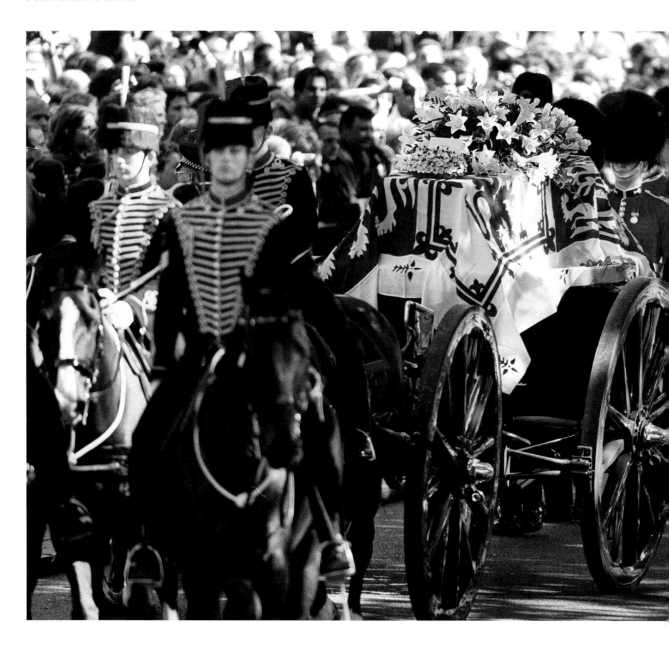

tive society, and that Diana, the girl from the old aristocracy who had married into royalty, epitomized it.

Yet the Princess was never in tune with the Iron Lady. "Who is society? There is no such thing," Thatcher told *Woman's Own* magazine in 1987. "There are individual men and women, and there are families." Thatcher's bracing doctrine of personal responsibility was always at odds with Diana's faith in the power of redemptive understanding, of allowing the weak to be weak. Her belief system very much included an entity called society, which rejected and marginalized people. "Someone has got to go out there and love people and show it," she said in her BBC interview.

By the time the Princess died, Thatcher was long gone, her pallid successor, John Major, had been vanquished, and Blair was in 10 Downing Street with a huge popular mandate to build a more inclusive, caring Britain. That agenda echoed Diana's. The Princess had two secret meetings with Blair before his election. According to Alastair Campbell's diaries, she told the intermediary who set up the meetings that "she would like to help [Labour] if she could." Diana had certainly made her mark on Campbell, who recorded that the Princess "had perfect skin and her whole face lit up when she spoke and there were moments when I had to fight to hear the words because I'm just lost in the beauty." These days Camp-

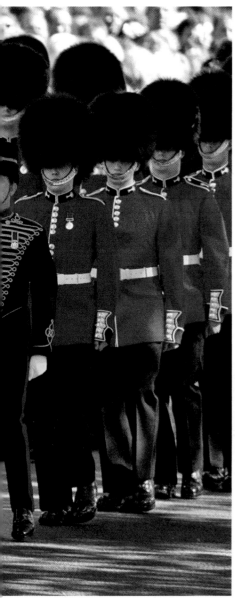

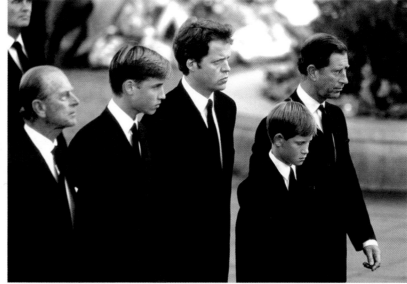

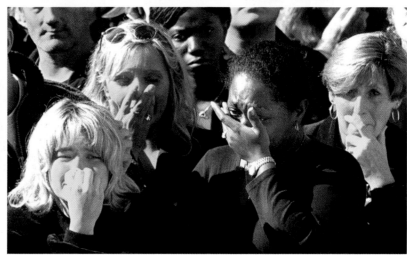

An estimated 3 million people lined the route of Diana's funeral procession (left) on Sept. 6, 1997; Prince Philip, Prince William, Earl Spencer, Prince Harry and Prince Charles, behind the cortège (top right); and mourners along the route

bell has a more sober assessment: "She was very small-p political. I have no idea if she would have ended up taking some kind of unofficial role with a Labour government, but I am sure she would have found a way of harnessing her own skills and popularity to the sense of Britain as a more modern and compassionate country."

We will never know if she would have achieved such a dispensation. But the fact that she was—undeniably—on occasion manipulative, deceitful and self-centered should not blind us to the fact that, during her 17 years in the limelight, she had grown as Britain had grown, changed as Britain had changed, and by the time she died, had something increas-

ingly vital to offer. Arbiter recalls a strange, muted, mournful night when he encountered a group of wheelchair users on their way to lay flowers at Kensington Palace. "They were saying, 'Who's going to speak for us, now?' They had a point. The disabled: Who's going to speak for them? The AIDS patients: Who's going to speak for them? The drug addicts, the down-and-outs, the homeless, the elderly? She was their voice and drew attention to their plight." Arbiter pauses. "She'd have made a good queen, you know. But that's it. She's gone."

Gone? As anyone who knows anything about the strains that make up modern Britain will tell you, that is very far from true.

Public Treasures

A cornerstone of Britain's identity, the royal family is itself a brand many businesses are keen to harness. Just who is getting happy and glorious as a result?

By William Lee Adams

O n the route from friendship to marriage, the Duke and Duchess of Cambridge transformed mere buildings into monuments of their decade-long romance. There's the University of St. Andrews, where they met as college students in 2001. There's St. James's Palace, where they held their engagement-day photo call in November 2010. And according to Katy Tucker, a 27-year old part-time actress who is leading today's London Walks "Royal Wedding Walk," there's Mahiki, the Polynesian-themed tiki bar where Wills drowned his sorrows during the couple's brief split in 2007. "He racked up an £11,000 ($17,600) bar tab," she tells the eight tourists who have braved freezing rain to take the two-hour walk. Continuing the tale widely reported in the tabloid press, she says, "He ended up slumped in the corner rather upset, but his friend dragged him on the dance floor for the Rolling Stones song 'You Can't Always Get What You Want.'" An American teenager laughs. Her mother claps. A psychiatrist

Crowds watch members of the Order of the Garter arrive for their annual service at St. George's Chapel in Windsor Castle

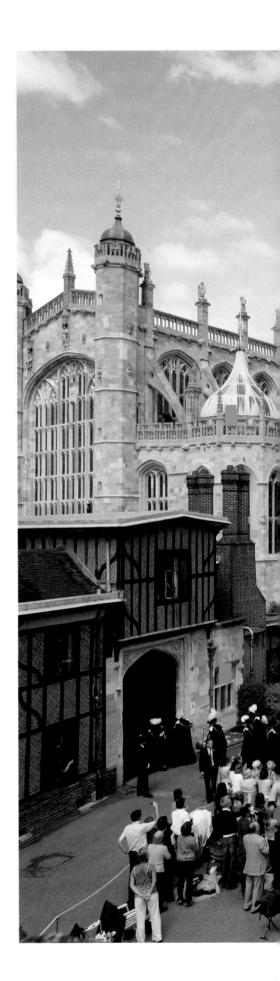

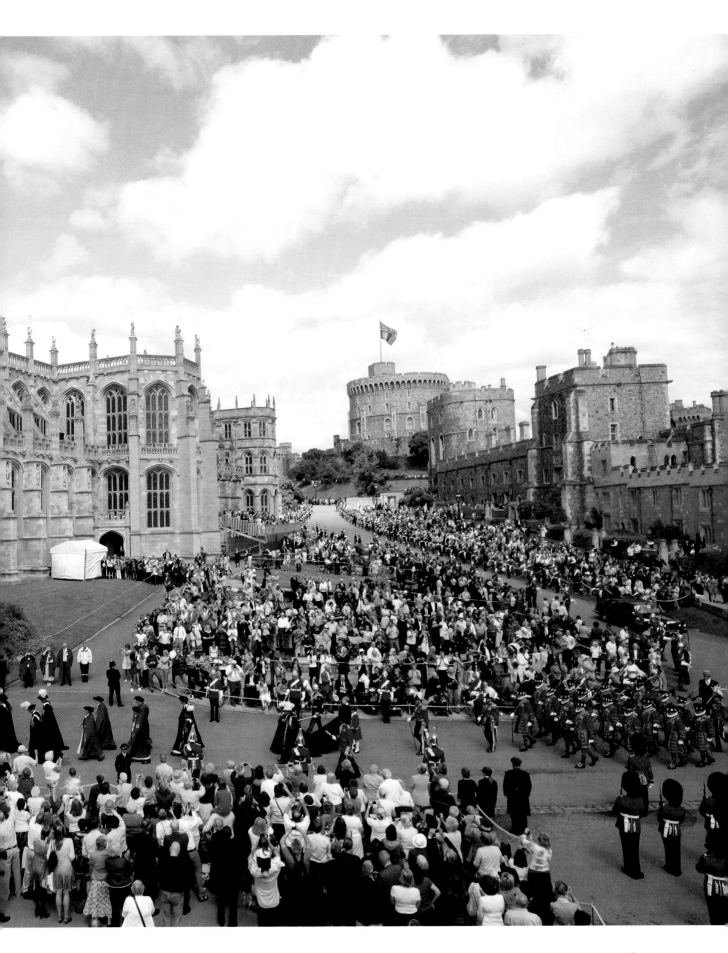

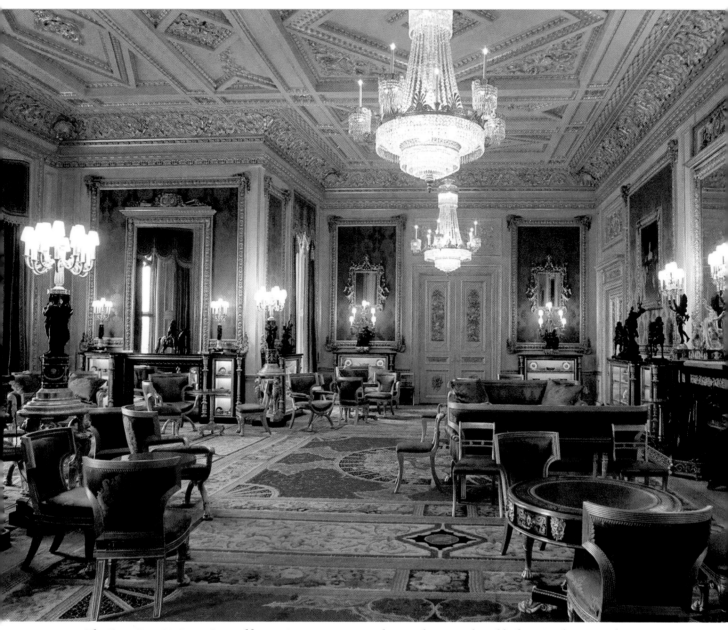

The Green Drawing Room is one of five semi-state rooms in Windsor Castle open to the public from October to March

from India pulls out his camera and takes a photo of a Polynesian idol stationed outside the bar.

The nuptials that eventually united Prince William and his commoner bride in holy matrimony set entrepreneurs' pulses racing. Big-name retailers produced knockoff engagement rings and Kate Middleton dresses; smaller operators found myriad ways to spread the love, from printing tea bags that bore cartoon images of the couple to walks and tailored tours. That countless businesses profit from the public's fascination with the monarchy isn't new. But royal extravaganzas—from Charles' and Diana's

wedding in 1981 to this summer's Diamond Jubilee marking the Queen's 60th year on the throne—give those operations a significant boost. Reiss, the London-based fashion chain, saw operating profits in its U.K. arm soar from $6.7 million in 2010 to $13.2 million in 2011—aided, they say, by Kate Middleton wearing their dresses before and after her wedding.

The royal family make the most of their own brand, too. The Royal Collection, which operates the Queen's gift shops and charges admission to sites like Buckingham Palace, reinvests its profits into maintaining royal residences and the Queen's

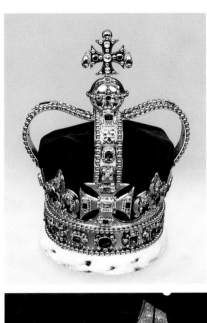
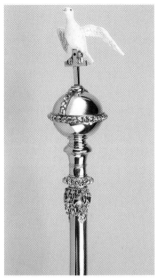
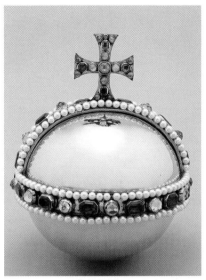
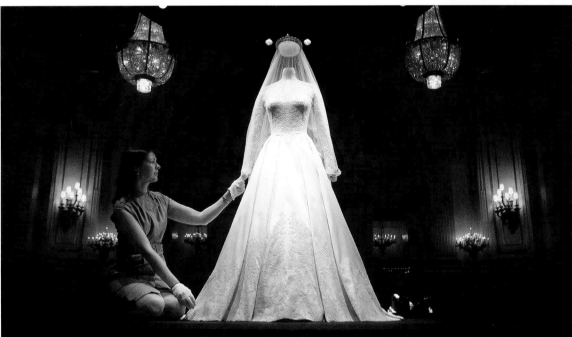

The crown jewels at the Tower of London (top); Kate Middleton's wedding gown on display at Buckingham Palace in 2011

art collection. Revenues amounted to $67 million in 2011—up 21% over 2010. And Prince Charles, a champion of sustainability and the organic-food movement, uses his Duchy Originals food line to promote those causes. He reinvests all profits into his Prince's Charities Foundation. "What makes London different from other European cities?" asks Tucker. "It's not the rain and the cold weather. It's our royal family. They're the most famous in the world."

That's true, and any benefits extend beyond the U.K. capital. But analyzing those benefits is even more difficult than totting up the total cost of the royals. Apart from the Queen's annual grant, which covers the expenses of her official state duties, there are other considerations. Taxpayers had to foot a $16 million security bill for the royal wedding. And according to the Bank of England, the additional public holiday marking the event contributed to a sharp decline in average hours worked and a 0.3% slump in manufacturing output during the second quarter of 2011. Mervyn King, the governor of the Bank of England, predicts that the additional holiday creating a four-day weekend to mark this summer's Diamond Jubilee will dampen economic activity rather than stimulate it.

The monarchy, no doubt, comes with a price tag. As royalists are keen to point out, based purely on Her Majesty's state funding, it amounts to just 82 cents per taxpayer, about the cost of a Queen Elizabeth postcard and considerably less than the $32 "It Should Have Been Me" royal wedding plate by London's KK Outlet. "I'm fairly convinced there is a positive effect on the economy of having a royal family, but trying to quantify that is nigh on impossible," says Philip Shaw, the chief economist at Investec, an asset-management firm in London. "What we don't know is whether the tourists would come here if the U.K. had no royal family."

That doesn't stop people from making big claims. According to VisitBritain, the official body that promotes tourism to the country, overseas residents who visit castles, cathedrals and historic homes "associated with the monarchy" pump $800 million into the economy annually. That's a difficult number to stand up—in part because those sites frequently have tenuous connections to the royals. But there does appear to have been a royal-wedding boost to tourism. In the three months to May 2011, foreigners made 7.8 million visits to the U.K.—a year-on-year jump of more than 10%. The festive mood may have encouraged them to spend bigger, too: over the same period, their expenditures rose by 7% to an estimated $6.4 billion. Accounting firm PwC

Clockwise from top left: A Princess Diana doll; Kate and Wills tea bags; a Prince Charles and Camilla wedding plate; a Queen Elizabeth-and-corgi doll; the official royal wedding loving cup; Knit Your Own Royal Wedding *dolls*

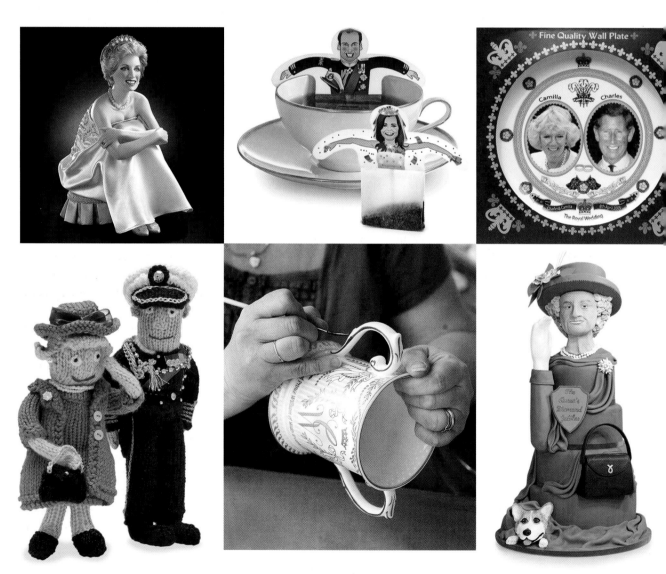

calculates that royal-wedding-related tourism contributed around $170 million to London as guests crowded hotels and restaurants. More than 600,000 people visited Buckingham Palace in August and September 2011, the two months of the year when it's open to the public during the Queen's annual visit to Scotland. That's more than in any year since the Queen first opened its doors to visitors in 1993—and they paid an admission fee of $29 each. During the Jubilee, it will be open longer. The country's national tourism agency predicts that, of the hundreds of millions of people overseas who watched the royal wedding, up to 4 million will eventually visit the U.K. as a result, bringing with them an extra $3.2 billion. "Pinning down these numbers is more of an art than a science," Shaw says.

Tourist sites are banking on another boost from the Queen's summer celebrations. Kensington Palace, Princess Diana's official residence until her death in 1997, closed for three months in order to undergo a $19 million transformation encompassing newly landscaped gardens, gift shops, and a permanent exhibit on Queen Victoria with artifacts such as Prince Albert's tongue scraper. When the Duke and Duchess of Cambridge move into private quarters in Kensington Palace as early as 2013, visitor numbers will likely pick up further.

Across town the Tower of London, the most popular royal attraction in the country, welcomed 2.4 million visitors last year—around 70% of them from abroad. Tens of thousands of Indian tourists come purely to see the Imperial Crown of India, which sparkles with more than 6,000 diamonds, and the Koh-I-Noor, once the largest-known diamond in the world, which colonial administrators seized for Queen Victoria in 1849. Anticipating that diamonds will be a tourist's best friend in the runup to the Diamond Jubilee, curators planned to unveil a new display for the crown jewels at the end of March.

The royal family has also helped transform the fortunes of independent artists and retailers—even if many of their items would make the Queen blush. Crown Jewels—a condom manufacturer—has released commemorative prophylactics ($13). "Like a royal wedding," its packaging reads, "intercourse with a loved one is an unforgettable occasion." They sold 10,000 packs in the first six months. David Emrey, who runs a small tea-towel company called ToDryFor in Oxford, shipped 2,000 tea towels in two months, priced at $16 each and featuring a corgi poking his head through a massive wedding ring. "Even now we still get repeat orders from abroad from people who wouldn't have heard of us otherwise," he says. And Fiona Goble released a book called *Knit Your Own Royal Wedding.* It quickly became the best-selling book on Amazon U.K. and has transformed her into the world's best-selling knitting writer. "I had no idea the idea would be so popular," she says. "We thought people who loved royalty and knitting would be something of a niche market."

Souvenirs commemorating the Diamond Jubilee itself seem tame in comparison. Queen Elizabeth smiles serenely on a series of mugs and dinner plates. Perhaps the wittiest item on offer is the Jubilee version of the Solar Queen ($27), a 6-in. replica of Elizabeth II holding a purse with a solar panel. "Place the Solar Queen in the sunlight and watch Her Majesty wave with a subtle twist of the wrist," its packaging says. "This gesture, cultivated over the centuries, is the true mark of royalty." Even the Middleton family sees an opportunity for the summer. Party Pieces, the party-supplies business that Kate's parents run, has introduced a Jubilee Celebrations line "to help you plan a spectacular party" to mark the Diamond Jubilee. It includes paper crowns ($8 for a four-pack) and coat-of-arms party cups ($5 for a 12-pack) that read "Long Live G&T!" It's natural that the business would want to celebrate. Party Pieces transformed the Middletons into multimillionaires, helping them send Kate to the private schools that ultimately led her to William. It now seems that the royals are inadvertently giving back to the business.

That story—of Kate's rise from well-to-do student to royal wife—partly explains why eight tourists on our walking tour have crowded around Jigsaw, a clothing chain for which the Duchess of Cambridge worked briefly as an accessories buyer after college. The tour guide discusses Kate's status as a fashion icon, and lists the various British retailers who rush to produce knockoff gowns every time she takes a turn on the red carpet. The Indian psychiatrist keeps taking pictures, which he plans to show to friends. "They like learning about these tours," he says, "and I like sharing." Fortunately for Britain's economy, he likes spending money, too.

The Stamp Of Her Influence

The Queen has one of the most famous images on the planet. In the age of free expression, her fixed expression is ubiquitous

By Belinda Luscombe

We know that the first Queen Elizabeth oversaw a period in which culture flourished, because Edmund Spenser's poem "The Faerie Queene" is about her, "that greatest Glorious Queene of Faerie lond," because her birth is mentioned in one of Shakespeare's plays (*Henry VIII*), and because she was painted by some of the greatest masters of the age. The second Queen Elizabeth has also inspired several classics, perhaps none more indelible than this from the Sex Pistols: "God Save the Queen / She ain't no human being / There is no future / in England's dreaming."

If the cultural artifacts inspired by the first Elizabeth seem more high-toned, the second Elizabeth wins hands down on quantity. Her current Majesty is very likely the most portrayed woman on the planet. Billions of stamps, millions of coins and notes, and hundreds of thousands of postcards bear her likeness. Her face, especially in profile, is recognized in every English-speaking land and is ubiquitous in several. Hers is not the exotic, come-hither face of a Marilyn or an Angelina. It's the face of distant historic authority, a literal figurehead, having no real

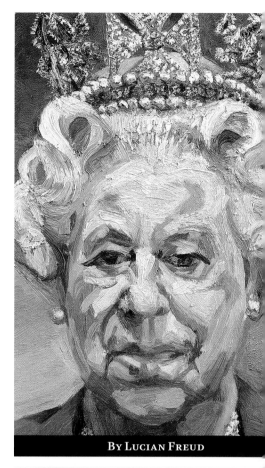

BY LUCIAN FREUD

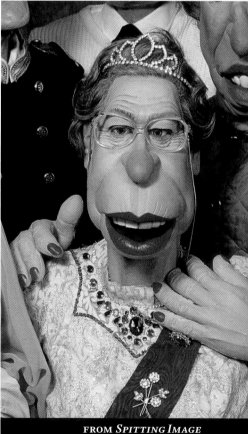

FROM *SPITTING IMAGE*

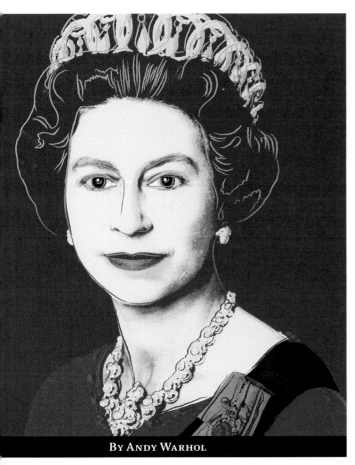

BY ANDY WARHOL

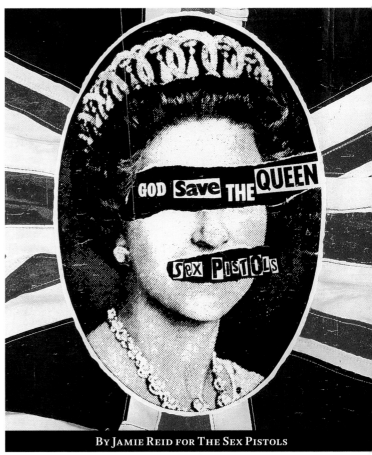

BY JAMIE REID FOR THE SEX PISTOLS

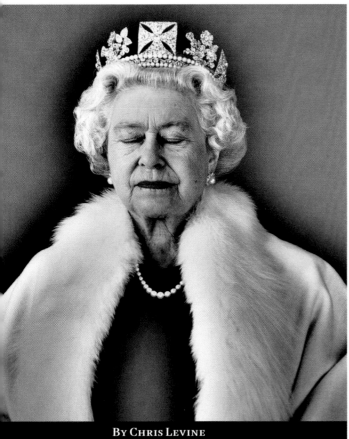

BY CHRIS LEVINE

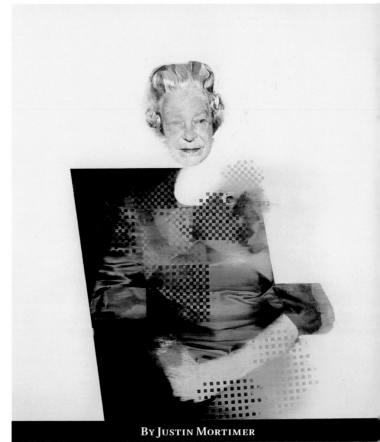

BY JUSTIN MORTIMER

power but oodles of symbolic supremacy.

Does ubiquity equal influence? The Queen does not inspire purchases the way Kate Moss or Kate Middleton might. She cannot give the sales of a certain brand of lipstick a fillip by casually dropping its name in conversation. But her complete lack of sex appeal or commercial appeal is actually the Queen's strength; it buttresses her rarer and more potent qualities: consistency and longevity. Whatever flavor of the month Kate Middleton may be, it's never going to be as durable as the Queen's regal vanilla.

Officially, Elizabeth II has sat for roughly 200 portraits by artists from Annie Leibovitz to Lucian Freud to hologram creator Chris Levine. She never gives her opinion on the results—at least not publicly—and seems to regard lending her time to artists as part of her cultural duty. The painters don't get to know their subject, because she can never be a subject. One artist—Justin Mortimer, whose portrayal stirred up controversy because it separated her head from her body—had two two-hour sittings with the Queen, mostly to take Polaroids and make sketches. "She sat very formally (like a Queen) in her chair and was chatting nonstop to her equerry," he recalled afterwards. The second session was more relaxed but not intimate. "We even talked. She was funny. " An-

Royal postcards were extremely popular, especially before TV, and Her Majesty's head, by law, has been on every British stamp since she ascended the throne

other sitting, for Australian entertainer-painter Rolf Harris, was filmed, but the small talk was tiny.

Of course, the Queen's official portraits, even those by masters such as Freud, are nowhere near as culturally relevant as her uncommissioned portrayals. She's vastly more influential as an icon than as a patron. As the apogee of all that is British and institutional and proper, Her Majesty serves as a useful target. Unchanging and unknowable, she is a perfect canvas on which to project the obsessions of the moment. Andy Warhol's silkscreen prints of Elizabeth, part of his *Reigning Queen* series of the mid '80s, treats her like any other celebrity, frozen in time and bright colors. Even earlier, Jamie Reid rendered her with a baby pin through her nose, like a '70s punk.

It was Reid, too, who created the 1977 cover for the Sex Pistols single "God Save the Queen," which has become part of a robust body of work that defaces the Queen's image as a shorthand for rebellion or antiestablishment passion. The British TV show *Spitting Image* (1984-96) used puppets to mock the royals, making them look them dim or harried. In the late '90s, another show, *The Royle Family,* followed the escapades and interactions of a family that mirrored the Windsors in uncanny ways—right down to the fact that both clans lived off the government—except the Royles were broke.

More recently the mock-the-Queen approach has fallen out of vogue, with such artists as Alison

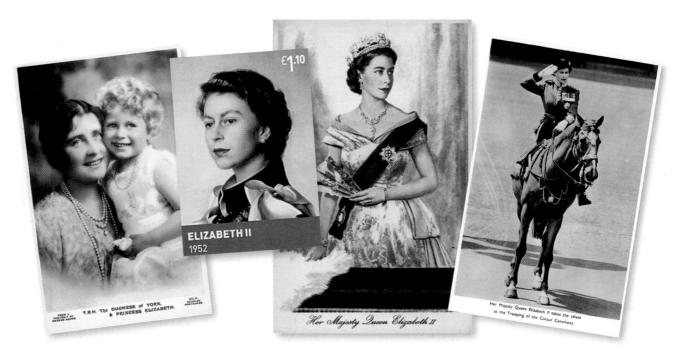

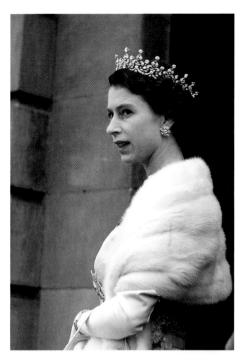
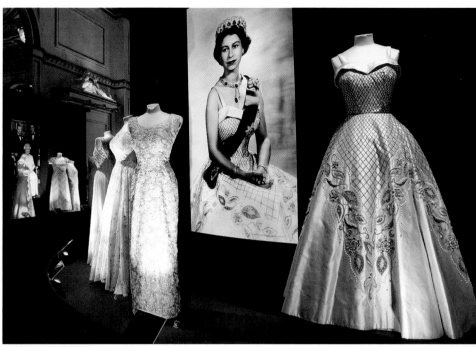
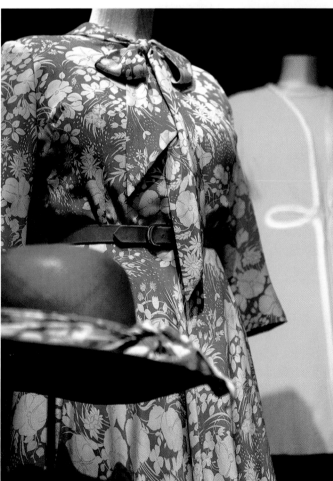
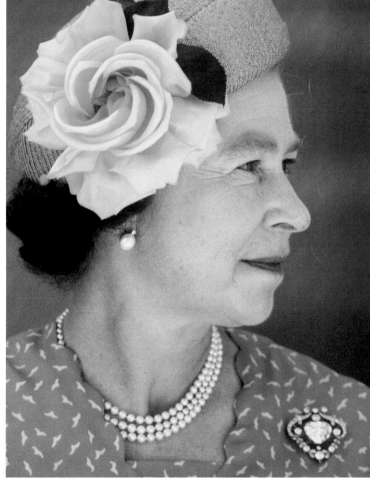

Clockwise from top left: the young Queen in 1954 in Australia; gowns from her trips to Commonwealth countries on display at Buckingham Palace in 2009; wearing her signature style in Tuvalu in 1982; two more ensembles from the 2009 show

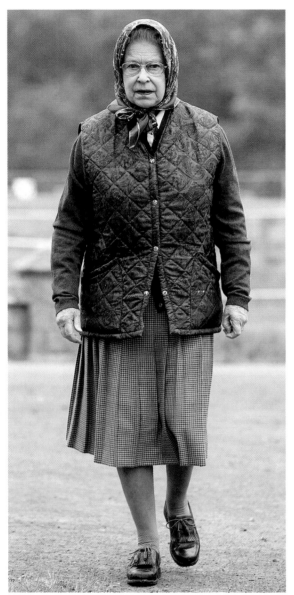
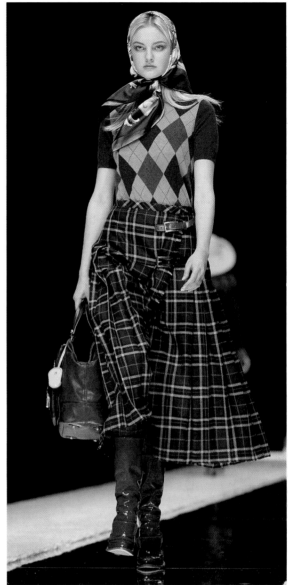

Left, the Queen on a dress-down day. Right, a look from Dolce & Gabbana's 2008 fall ready-to-wear collection, in homage

Jackson examining instead the strangeness of the public appetite for intimate or embarrassing details about the royal family. Jackson gets lookalike actors to pose as, say, the Queen on the toilet reading a newspaper and photographs them in paparazzo style. The juxtaposition is uncomfortable, confronting readers with their own voyeurism: In a world full of artifice masquerading as reality, what images of the western world's most gilded family do we seek out and create?

Perhaps the most interesting evolution of the Queen's cultural impact can be seen in the fashion industry. Her clothing choices, never considered avant-garde or even fashion forward, can be most generously described as safe. Under the risible head-

line "Elizabethan look may capture Fashion World," the *Pittsburgh Press* of February 1952 praised the Queen's fashion choices and her "dainty waist and slim hips" but noted that Norman Hartnell, one of the couturiers to the Crown, said that "no member of the royal family intends to influence fashion." If that was her aim, it has been one of the Queen's most successful and lasting campaigns.

The point of Her Maj's wardrobe is pretty much to wear what no one else will. She dons bright colors and bold prints so she can be easily spotted in a crowd. This tends to send the royal dresser to a lot of fuchsias, primrose yellows and purples—and so much the better if those colors aren't fashionable.

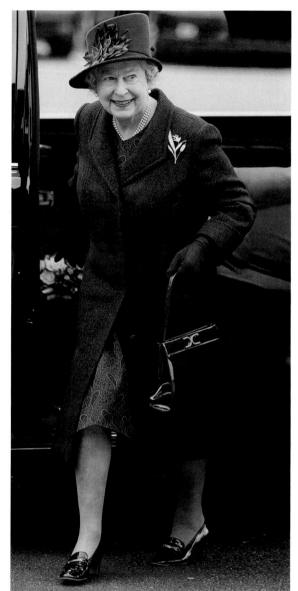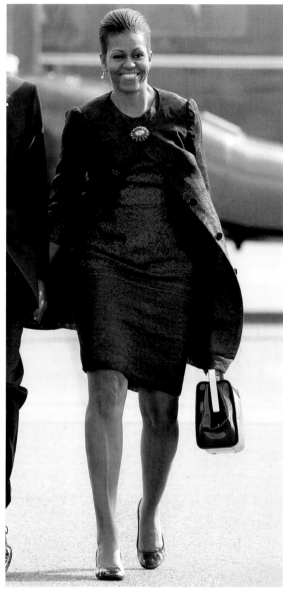

Purple coat, purple frock, brooch, sensible shoes and bag: Michelle Obama seems to have taken a leaf from the royal lookbook

Because she cannot under any circumstances be underdressed, the Queen will often wear matching hat, coat and gloves. For a long time this extreme matchiness was considered the leading edge of frumpiness. But over the years, the Queen's highly coordinated, color-saturated look began to appeal to other women, particularly those in positions of prominence without power. Michelle Obama wears similar hues and bright patterns (witness the matching yellow dress-and-coat ensembles she wore to her husband's inauguration and Nobel Peace Prize ceremonies). Carla Bruni, the first lady of France, has regularly rocked blouses tied with a bow, like those the Queen favors. The trickle-down effect has spilled over onto women who like to be contrary: Uber-hip British model Agyness Deyn cites the sovereign as her fashion icon. "The Queen dresses all matching," noted Japanese *Vogue* editor-at-large Anna Dello Russo. "What incredible impact that has. No one else dresses all in pink without looking hilarious, but she does. She pulls it off." Even the Queen's conspicuously dowdy casual wear, with its range of headscarves, wool skirts and knee socks, has been aped; it was the inspiration for Dolce & Gabbana's fall 2008 ready-to-wear line. All this must be very reassuring to a monarch in her twilight years. She doesn't have to change to keep up with the times. If she just stays as she is, the times will circle back to her.

About the Authors

William Lee Adams is a TIME staff writer based in London. Since joining in 2007, he has picked up bylines in 15 countries, reporting from drug houses in Romania, maximum-security prisons in Norway and the world's largest song contest for kids, in Belarus, among other places.

Howard Chua-Eoan became TIME's news director in 2000 after 17 years at the magazine as a writer and editor, as well as a brief stint at *People*. He was TIME's weekend editor on duty when news broke of the accident that took Princess Diana's life. He edited and co-wrote stories, organized the 16-hour effort that completely revamped that week's issue, and was deeply involved in the following week's commemorative issue.

Belinda Luscombe is an editor-at-large at TIME. She has written and edited culture stories at the magazine since 1996. At the age of 10, she got lost for hours in the huge crowd that amassed to see the Queen open the Opera House in her hometown, Sydney. She has never fully recovered.

Catherine Mayer is TIME's Europe editor and the author of the 2011 book *Amortality: The Pleasures and Perils of Living Agelessly.* A longtime London-based correspondent, she has been covering Britain and the Windsors since 1993. Her first encounter with royalty occurred at age 7, when she played the recorder for the Queen Mother. In 2010 she won the Foreign Press Association award for Story of the Year for a piece about Prime Minister David Cameron's recalibration of Britain's special relationship with the U.S.

Allison Pearson is an international bestselling author and a columnist on the *London Daily Telegraph.* Allison's first novel, *I Don't Know How She Does It,* about the crazy struggles of a working mom, has been translated into 32 languages and in 2011 became a movie starring Sarah Jessica Parker. Her critically acclaimed second novel, *I Think I Love You,* about a teenage girl and her pop idol, is in development as a musical. She lives in Cambridge, England, with her family and is working on the sequel to *I Don't Know How She Does It.*

Credits